The Mechanics of Divine Foreknowledge and Providence

Bloomsbury Studies in Philosophy of Religion

Series Editor:
Stewart Goetz

Editorial Board:
Thomas Flint, Robert Koons, Alexander Pruss, Charles Taliaferro,
Roger Trigg, David Widerker, Mark Wynn

Titles in the Series

The Mechanics of Divine Foreknowledge and Providence

A Time-Ordering Account

T. Ryan Byerly

B L O O M S B U R Y

NEW YORK · LONDON · NEW DELHI · SYDNEY

Bloomsbury Academic

An imprint of Bloomsbury Publishing Inc

1385 Broadway	50 Bedford Square
New York	London
NY 10018	WC1B 3DP
USA	UK

www.bloomsbury.com

Bloomsbury is a registered trade mark of Bloomsbury Publishing Plc

First published 2014

Library of Congress Cataloging-in-Publication Data
Byerly, T. Ryan.
The mechanics of divine foreknowledge and providence :
a time-ordering account / T. Ryan Byerly. – 1st [edition].
pages cm
Includes bibliographical references and index.
ISBN 978-1-62356-559-6 (hardback : alk. paper) 1. God (Christianity)–Omniscience.
2. Free will and determinism. 3. Philosophical theology.
4. Providence and government of God–Christianity. I. Title.
BT131.B94 2014
231'.5–dc23
2014008260

ISBN: HB: 978-1-6235-6559-6
ePDF: 978-1-6235-6788-0
ePub: 978-1-6235-6686-9

Typeset by Integra Software Services Pvt. Ltd.
Printed and bound in the United States of America

Contents

Acknowledgments

There are both individuals and organizations who deserve my sincere thanks for their generous support of my work on this book.

First, I thank the members of my family, especially my dear wife, Meghan, who patiently allowed me to pursue the research and writing of this work, believing it to be of value for both me and the profession. I am grateful, Love, for your most constant encouragement.

Next, I thank those who took the time to discuss with me the ideas which ultimately led to this book when they were still in very nascent form. The key idea about time-ordering was born out of casual conversation with Dan Johnson, and I would not have pursued developing this idea further without later conversation with Chris Tweedt.

Third, I thank the audience members who heard me present parts of the work and offered helpful feedback. Part of Chapter 4 was presented at the Analytic Theology Summer School in Munich, Germany, in 2012, and another part of the chapter was presented at the National Endowment for the Humanities Summer Seminar on Metaphysics and Mind in 2013. Part of Chapter 5 was presented at the Midwest Regional Meeting of the Society of Christian Philosophers in 2013. I am grateful to audience members at each of these presentations, especially Patrick Todd, Kevin Sharpe, Adam Pelser, and David Alexander, for their helpful feedback.

Fourth, I thank those institutions which either directly or indirectly supported my efforts in writing this book. A summer stipend from the Center for Philosophy of Religion at the University of Notre Dame enabled me to continue sustained work on the topic of divine time-ordering. And, participating in the 2012 St. Thomas Summer Seminar in Philosophy of Religion offered me an opportunity to further pursue research on freedom and foreknowledge which ultimately led to several papers on the topic as well as this book.

Finally, I thank the members of the team at Bloomsbury Press, especially series editor Stewart Goetz and publisher Haaris Naqvi, for their leadership in producing and distributing this text.

Introduction

If God knew long ago with perfection what I will do each day for the rest of my life, then how could it be that what I do each day for the rest of my life is genuinely up to *me*? On the other hand, if much of what I will do each day for the rest of my life *is* genuinely up to me, then how could it be that *God* is in control of these things I will do? These two questions, or questions much like them, lie at the heart of perennial debates in philosophical theology which are at once among the most difficult and the most rewarding within the discipline. The debates to which they are central have endured at least since the third century, and the questions themselves are no less pertinent than they are ancient.

The purpose of this book is to contribute to contemporary philosophical discussions of the questions posed earlier by articulating and defending a novel account of the mechanics of infallible divine foreknowledge—an answer to the question of *how* divine foreknowledge might be achieved—which does not require that human actions are causally determined. In other words, I will propose an answer to the question of how it is that God could know with perfection what I will do each day for the rest of my life where the method whereby God comes to know these things does not imply that my actions are causally determined. If indeed there is such a method available to God, it would be quite significant. For, as I show in Part I, even the very best arguments for the incompatibility of human freedom and divine foreknowledge succeed only if the mechanics whereby God secures his foreknowledge requires causal determinism. Thus, we are in a position to know that divine foreknowledge and human freedom are incompatible on the basis of these arguments only if we are in a position to know that God achieves foreknowledge via a method which requires causal determinism. However, I will argue that we are in no such position to know that God achieves foreknowledge in a way that requires causal determinism. For, there are methods of achieving such foreknowledge, such as the one I will develop and defend in Part II of this text, which do not require causal determinism. And, nothing we know implies that these methods are not the ones used by God.

The account of the mechanics of divine foreknowledge I will advocate does not address only the first question, however; it also addresses the second question concerning human freedom and divine providence. For, the theory I shall develop concerning how God achieves infallible foreknowledge is at once also a theory about how God exercises control over the happenings of the cosmos. Indeed, it provides the resources for articulating a careful version of divine concurrentism according to which God and creatures are both intimately causally involved in the production of those effects attributable to creatures. Thus, the book aims to produce a theory of divine providence which is compatible with the existence of creaturely freedom and which makes available a method for God to know infallibly everything that will unfold in the history of the world, including those actions performed freely by human beings.

The book begins in Chapter 1 with a detailed presentation of an argument which has dominated contemporary philosophical discussion of the relationship between human freedom and divine foreknowledge: the foreknowledge argument. After carefully presenting this argument, I provide the reader with a critical, up-to-date introduction to the available options for responding to this argument by denying one or another of its premises or inferences. While this discussion includes much material which can be found in good encyclopedia entries on the topic, it also includes discussion of important work which tends to be neglected in these avenues as well as a several novel contributions to the debate.

Chapter 2 presents my argument that the foreknowledge argument and others like it can succeed only if the mechanics whereby God achieves foreknowledge requires causal determinism. To anticipate very briefly, I argue that while the existence of infallible divine foreknowledge might *show* that human actions are not done freely, the existence of infallible divine foreknowledge *couldn't* be what *makes* human actions unfree. Something else, something that the existence of infallible divine foreknowledge requires, must do this; and, the best candidate is that infallible divine foreknowledge requires causal determinism. Thus, the foreknowledge argument can succeed in showing that infallible divine foreknowledge is incompatible with human freedom only if the mechanics whereby this foreknowledge is achieved requires causal determinism. Accordingly, we must attend to the question of whether there is good reason to think that the mechanics whereby divine foreknowledge is achieved requires causal determinism. I conclude Chapter 2 by presenting the best argument I know of in favor of the conclusion that the mechanics of divine foreknowledge *does* require causal determinism. The argument is a very powerful inductive argument which relies upon a key inductive generalization. The inductive generalization moves from the claim that *all ways of attaining foreknowledge we know of* involve drawing inferences on the basis of the believer's knowledge of the past and laws of nature to the claim that *all ways of attaining foreknowledge* involve drawing inferences on the basis of the believer's knowledge of the past and laws of nature. The remainder of the book is dedicated to responding to this argument.

In Chapter 3 I begin my response to the aforementioned inductive argument. I consider, first, whether one might appeal to considerations about human ignorance of ways of achieving knowledge in order to respond to this argument in a manner much like that used by skeptical theists to respond to the evidential problem of evil. This possibility naturally suggests itself, given the similarity between the inductive generalization that figures into the inductive argument articulated at the end of Chapter 2 and those inductive generalizations that figure into leading presentations of the evidential problem of evil. After considering this first possible kind of response, I go on to discuss the importance of telling conciliatory stories about the mechanics of infallible divine foreknowledge with one or another degree of plausibility in which God achieves infallible foreknowledge without causal determinism. The existence of such stories, I argue, can blunt the force of the inductive argument from Chapter 2.

Chapter 3 concludes by considering canonical conciliatory stories and evaluating to what extent they succeed at delivering a plausible mechanics of foreknowledge which does not require causal determinism. I maintain that there are weaknesses in leading available stories, such as Molinism. My own story aims to remedy these weaknesses.

Part II is dedicated to developing and defending my own conciliatory story concerning the mechanics of foreknowledge, one that appeals to God's ordering of the times. In Chapter 4, I carefully articulate the story, defend its coherence and plausibility given theism, and argue that it does not require causal determinism. An important component of the argument for the latter conclusion involves arguing that the way causal determinism has been defined in recent philosophical literature needs reworking. This argument should be of interest to anyone working on the topic of freedom and determinism generally, not just those interested in free will within the philosophy of religion. Once causal determinism is properly defined, there is good reason to think that my model of the mechanics of infallible divine foreknowledge does not require it.

Chapter 5 discusses how the model of the mechanics of divine foreknowledge I develop in Chapter 4 in fact simultaneously provides a general theory of providence. It is a theory which provides the resources for defending a version of divine concurrentism against an important objection which any concurrentist view must overcome—an objection based on overdetermination. I show, further, that the time-ordering theory of providence also provides a ready solution to the problem of divine governance of indeterministic processes. These features of the time-ordering view make it only more attractive from the perspective of theism.

The final chapter, Chapter 6, examines the value and future of both the general conciliatory story strategy outlined in Chapter 3 as well as the time-ordering implementation of this strategy in Chapters 4 and 5. I defend three conclusions. First, the conciliatory story strategy, as well as the time-ordering implementation of this strategy, meets the necessary criteria for a successful response to the foreknowledge argument outlined in Chapter 1—criteria arguably not satisfied by any response to the foreknowledge argument which involves denying a premise or inference in the argument. Second, representative attempts to provide a simpler response to the foreknowledge argument than the one I develop here, where these responses also do not involve denying a premise or inference in the argument, fail. Third, there is good reason to think that there are adequate responses to the most significant objections to the conciliatory story strategy and the time-ordering implementation of this strategy. Given these conclusions, the value of the strategic response to the foreknowledge argument offered here is considerable and its future is bright.

I conclude this introduction with a remark about my hope for this book. My hope is that this book will generate increased interest among philosophers in discussing the question of *how* divine foreknowledge and providence might be achieved. Unfortunately, in far too many recent discussions, this question is overlooked as philosophers have instead focused their efforts rather exclusively on the foreknowledge argument discussed in Chapter 1 of this text. While I encourage discussion of this argument as there is much fascinating material there to learn, I caution that the questions which are driving the present inquiry are in fact formulated as questions about mechanics. The inquirer asked, "*how* could it be that what I do each day for the rest of my life is genuinely up to me?" and "*how* could it be that God is in control of these things I will do?" Even if contemporary philosophers do not find ultimately attractive the particular answer to these questions, which the current text defends, I hope they will nonetheless turn their attention more explicitly to the questions. And I hope this book plays a significant role in leading them to do so.

Part One

From the Existence of Divine Foreknowledge to Its Mechanics

1

The Foreknowledge Argument

The Introduction to this text began with two questions—one about the relationship between human freedom and divine foreknowledge and one about the relationship between human freedom and divine providence. In Part I, my focus is on the question concerning freedom and foreknowledge: "If God knew long ago with perfection what I will do each day for the rest of my life, then how could it be that what I do each day for the rest of my life is genuinely up to *me*?"

Discussion of this question among contemporary philosophers has tended to focus on a certain argument that attempts to show that an infallible God's having long ago possessed exhaustive foreknowledge implies that no human being performs any action she performs freely. For ease of reference, I will call this argument *the foreknowledge argument*. In this chapter, I present a careful version of the foreknowledge argument, compare it with two similar fatalistic arguments, and offer an up-to-date discussion of responses to it which reject one of its premises or inferences. My goal will be to establish criteria for judging a response to the foreknowledge argument to be successful and to cast significant doubt on whether any response to the argument which rejects one of its premises or inferences satisfies these criteria. One might conclude from this that the foreknowledge argument is a success. But I think that judgment is premature. Rather, my hope is to pique the reader's interest in the prospects for developing a successful response to the argument which does not involve rejecting one of the argument's key premises or inferences.

1. The foreknowledge argument

The aim of the present section is to present and explain a leading version of the foreknowledge argument, one which has been called by some authors the best version of this argument.[1] As we will see, the foreknowledge argument makes salient a puzzle which is generated by two motivations which many religious believers in the west have shared a motivation on the one hand to maintain a commitment to divine cognitive perfection and a motivation on the other hand to uphold a certain kind of freedom for human beings.

---

[1]   See Zagzebski (1996, Chapter 1).

We can start with the following informal presentation of the foreknowledge argument, which we will later compare to informal versions of parallel arguments for causal fatalism and logical fatalism:

> There's nothing I can now do about what anyone, including God, believed long ago. But, then, if God believed long ago that I will do certain things each day for the rest of my life, and God cannot be mistaken, then there's nothing I can now do about these things, either. So, if God believed long ago that I will do certain things each day for the rest of my life and God cannot be mistaken, then whether I do those things isn't up to me.

This informal line of reasoning is likely to strike a chord with any reader who has given much thought to the question of whether infallible divine foreknowledge and human freedom are compatible. And, it is not far off from the most carefully developed contemporary statements of the foreknowledge argument.

The informal version of the foreknowledge argument just presented can be precisified into a formal version which makes its key logical features and commitments explicit. The formal version of the foreknowledge argument I will present is a conditional proof. Assuming that an infallible God believed some claim in the distant past concerning an arbitrarily selected human being's future action, the argument attempts to show that this action could not be done freely. Thus, infallible divine foreknowledge and human free action are incompatible.

We can get the formal version of the foreknowledge argument started by adopting two suppositions which we will assume for the purpose of providing the conditional proof. The first supposition concerns a divine forebelief:

(1) God believed at t_1 that Elizabeth would sing a love sonnet to John at t_{100}.

Let t_1 refer to a time long, long before time t_{100}, even before Elizabeth or John came into being. Stipulating that t_1 is earlier than t_{100} is what makes the foreknowledge argument an argument about *fore*knowledge—or, more precisely, *fore*belief. As indicated already, the selection of Elizabeth and her action of singing a love sonnet is entirely arbitrary.

The second supposition we need concerns divine infallibility. What we will focus on is a requirement for divine infallibility which says that God *can't* be wrong in his beliefs.[2] It is tempting to explain this idea as follows: necessarily, if God believes something, it is so. The motivations for claiming that God meets this requirement for infallibility typically derive from strong commitments concerning divine cognitive perfection. For example, classical theism holds that it is central to divine cognitive perfection that God is omniscient. This is to say, roughly, that for every proposition p, if p, then God knows that p. Further, it isn't just that God simply *happens* to know every proposition that is the case but rather that he couldn't have failed to know each

---

[2]   Infallibility likely requires more than what (2) claims of God. For what else it might require, see Lewis (1996).

proposition that is the case. Thus, *necessarily*, for every proposition p, if p, then God knows p. However, plausibly, any person who knows a proposition p both believes p and *doesn't* believe not-p. So, given the classical theist's view that God couldn't fail to know each proposition which is the case, it follows that, necessarily, for any proposition p, if p, then God believes p and God *doesn't* believe not-p. And from this claim the requirement of divine infallibility stated earlier can be proven: namely, it is necessarily the case that if God believes p, then p.[3]

The claim that, necessarily, if God believes p then p is not quite the claim that we will use for our argument, however. Instead, we will use a claim which focuses both more narrowly on divine beliefs *about the actions of human agents at times* and more specifically on divine beliefs *held at times*. Informally, the claim we will focus on says: necessarily, if God believes at any time that some human agent performs an action at some time, then that agent does perform that action at that time. Formally, we can express our second supposition as follows:

(2) $\Box_L$ $\forall$t, t', S, A (God believes at t that S does A at t' $\rightarrow$ S does A at t')

In (2), "$\Box_L$" indicates logical necessity, "$\rightarrow$" indicates the material "if-then" conditional, and "$\forall$" indicates the universal quantifier. Thus, in English, (2) says: "it is logically necessary that, for any times t and t', any human agent S and any action A, if God believes at t that S does A at t', then S does A at t'."

There are several further notes I should offer to help explain the meaning of (2) and to explain why (2), rather than some similar claim about infallibility, is being put to work in the foreknowledge argument. First, I use $\Box_L$ and speak of *logical* necessity to distinguish the necessity here from other kinds of necessities. I use the language of "logical necessity" and "logical possibility" to indicate that a thing is necessary or possible in an absolutely unqualified way, in contrast to things which are possible or necessary *subject to certain qualifications*. An example of a claim which is necessarily the case in this unqualified way is the claim *all green things are colored*. It is impossible that this claim be false, not just subject to certain qualifications, but absolutely. It is always and under every condition impossible for something to be green and non-colored, not just impossible relative to certain times or certain conditions. (2) claims that it is necessary in this unqualified way—necessary at all times and under all conditions—that if God believes at any time a claim about what an agent does at some time, then this agent does what God believes he or she does at that time. The necessity involved here is the same sort of necessity involved in the classical theist's claim that God is necessarily such that for any proposition p, if p, then God knows p.

---

[3] Proof: Suppose that necessarily, for any proposition p, if p then God believes p and God doesn't believe not-p, in accordance with what was said in the text about essential omniscience. And suppose, for *reductio*, that possibly God believes a proposition p when not-p. Given that not-p, it will follow that God believes not-p and that God doesn't believe not-not-p. Further, plausibly, if God doesn't believe not-not-p then God doesn't believe p—i.e., God is competent at applying the inference rule of double negation. But now we have a contradiction—God believes p and God doesn't believe p. So, we must reject our supposition—that it is possible that God believes a proposition p when not-p.

Second, as highlighted earlier, (2) concerns divine beliefs *held at times* rather than simply divine beliefs. The reason for focusing attention in (2) on divine beliefs *held at times* is that (1) likewise focuses on a divine belief *held at a time*. Prima facie, someone who is willing to suppose, with (1), that God holds beliefs at times and who is also attracted to the view that God can't go wrong in his beliefs, should be happy to endorse supposition (2).

Finally, it is noteworthy that (2) focuses only on divine beliefs *about what agents do at times* rather than divine beliefs *about anything whatsoever*. For instance, we might have imagined that instead of (2), the following claim could have been used in the foreknowledge argument: necessarily, if God believes any proposition p at any time t, then p. Apart from the fact that, following (1), the foreknowledge argument is itself already focused only on a belief about what an agent does at a time, it turns out that there are also theoretical advantages to restricting (2) to divine beliefs about what agents do, or at least what happens, at times. For, there are objections which would face (2) if it concerned divine beliefs about just anything, objections that are overcome given the restrictions found in (2) as it is stated. To see this, one needs only to observe that there are some philosophers who have been attracted to the view that certain propositions change their truth-values.[4] For example, it may be true at one time that Socrates is bent and not true at some later time that Socrates is bent. Other propositions, such as Socrates is bent *at time t* more plausibly, do not change their truth-values. If Socrates is bent *at t*, then at every time it is true that Socrates is bent *at t*. A person who thought that some, though not all, propositions can change their truth-values would be unlikely to explain divine infallibility by claiming that necessarily, for every proposition p, if God believes p at any time, then p. Such a person may nonetheless be quite happy saying that necessarily if God believes at any time that an agent S does an action A *at t*, then S does A *at t*. Thus, restricting the objects of divine beliefs in (2) to propositions concerning what agents do at times has a significant theoretical advantage over a similar claim about divine infallibility concerning divine beliefs about *just anything*.

Claims (1) and (2) are the two suppositions of the foreknowledge argument. The remainder of the argument attempts to show that suppositions (1) and (2) imply that Elizabeth's singing her love sonnet to John at t_{100} is not something she does freely. In order to do so, the argument will need to make several additional claims about the nature of the past, necessity, and freedom.

Let us begin with a key claim about the past, a claim sometimes called the Principle of the Necessity of the Past or the Principle of the Fixity of the Past:

(3) $\forall t, t', x \,[(x \text{ obtains at } t \text{ and } t < t') \rightarrow (\square_A \text{ at } t' \text{ that } x \text{ obtains at } t)]$

Here "$\forall$" is used as before, while "$<$" is used to indicate "is earlier than" and "$\square_A$" is used to indicate "it is accidentally necessary that". Thus, in English, (3) claims: "For all times t and t′ and each state of affairs x, if x obtains at t and t is earlier than t′, then

---

[4]   See Prior (1996) and Merricks (2009).

it is accidentally necessary at t′ that x obtained at t." A bit more intuitively and less cumbersomely, (3) affirms that every state of affairs that obtained in the past is now necessary—accidentally necessary.[5]

The key to understanding claim (3) and its plausibility is to understand the notion of accidental necessity, $\Box_A$. Accidental necessity, in contrast to logical necessity, is a sort of necessity subject to certain conditions—chiefly temporal conditions. Its distinguishing mark is that it is a necessity relativized to times. Nothing is accidentally necessary *unqualifiedly*; what is accidentally necessary is necessary only *at some time or other*.[6,7]

Is there anything that is necessary at some times but not at others, possible at some times but not at others? Intuitive examples suggest an affirmative answer. For example, given that Lincoln was shot, it is not now possible that Lincoln has not been shot. Lincoln's not having been shot is now impossible. Of course, there may have been a time, say, on the night when Lincoln was making his way to the theater, when it *was* possible for Lincoln not to be shot. It seems to follow then that there is a state of affairs, that of Lincoln's not being shot, which was at one time possible, but is no longer possible. Conversely, Lincoln's being shot is an example of something which *has* to be at some times—i.e., it is necessary at some times—such as the present, but didn't *have* to be at other times. Thus, there is some sort of necessity which is accidental—a necessity relative to times.

Examples of past states of affairs are very useful in illustrating the concept of accidental necessity. And this may be for very good reason. For, it may be that *every* past state of affairs is accidentally necessary. Everything that has happened in the past *now* cannot fail to have happened. But this does not seem to be the case with the future. At least certain future happenings seem as if they now could happen and now could not happen. It seems as if it is now possible for them to happen and now possible for them not to happen. That the past is accidentally necessary may then be part of what sets it apart from the future. The idea that the past indeed is now necessary simply in virtue of being past is encapsulated in (3).

Given (1) and (3), we are now able to make a key inference. We can infer:

(4) $\Box_A$ at t_{100} that God believes at t_1 that Elizabeth will sing a love sonnet to John at t_{100}.

Since God's belief referred to here is said to have occurred at t_1 and t_1 is earlier than t_{100}, it follows from the Principle of the Necessity of the Past that God's having held

---

[5] Here I speak loosely calling states of affairs and not just propositions "necessary". I will continue to do this on occasion as nothing important will turn on it.

[6] See Zagzebski (1996) for a fuller discussion of this historical development of the concept of accidental necessity.

[7] It is also important to keep in mind that what we have in view here is some sort of *metaphysical* possibility and necessity and not *epistemic* possibility and necessity. On the latter, see Egan and Weatherson (2011).

this belief at t_1 is accidentally necessary at t_{100}. That is, it follows that God's having held this belief at t_1 is accidentally necessary at t_{100}, so long as we assume that God's belief is something which *obtained* at t_{100}. We will return to this idea of God's belief obtaining later.

The next claim needed for our argument is a transfer principle which tells us something about the logic of $\Box_A$. We can put the principle, which I will sometimes refer to as the transfer of Accidental Necessity principle, as follows:

(5) $\forall p, q, t \ [(\Box_A \text{ at t that } p \text{ and } \Box_L(p{\rightarrow}q)){\rightarrow} \Box_A \text{ at t that } q]$

Premise (5) says that for all propositions p and q and all times t, if it is accidentally necessary at t that p and if it is logically necessary that if p then q, then it is accidentally necessary at t that q. Less cumbersomely, (5) says that anything entailed by that which is accidentally necessary at a time is itself accidentally necessary at that time. Premise (5) is rarely challenged because it so closely resembles other transfer-of-necessity principles which are widely thought to be true. Such transfer principles are found, for example, in every axiomatic system for logical possibility and necessity.[8]

Our next observation is to note another inference that is now available on the basis of the components of our argument:

(6) $\Box_A$ at t_{100} that Elizabeth sings a love sonnet to John at t_{100}.

Claim (6) follows from (2), (4), and (5). For, per claim (4), God's belief at t_1 that Elizabeth will sing at t_{100} is accidentally necessary at t_{100}; per claim (2), God's believing at t_1 that Elizabeth will sing at t_{100} entails that she sings at t_{100}; and per claim (5), that which is entailed by what is accidentally necessary is itself accidentally necessary.

We are nearing the conclusion of our argument. The final claim we need before reaching our conclusion is a principle about freedom. The principle says:

(7) $\forall S, A, t \ (\Box_A \text{ at t that S does A at t} \rightarrow \text{S's doing A at t is not done freely})$

Claim (7) tells us that for all agents S, actions A and times t, if it is accidentally necessary at t that S does A at t, then S's doing A at t is not done freely.

The primary motivation for affirming (7) is that it is a version of the Principle of Alternate Possibilities. The Principle of Alternate Possibilities claims, roughly, that if a person performs an action A freely, she could have done otherwise than perform A.[9] By contraposition, this says that if a person could not have done otherwise than perform an action A—i.e., her performing action A was necessary—then she did not perform A freely. Claim (7) simply specifies a certain kind of necessity for this principle. It claims that if a person's performing an action A was *accidentally* necessary, then her

---

[8]   See Sider (2010).
[9]   There are other versions of the principle, as emphasized in Timpe (2006a). See further discussion in the text later where the rejection of (7) is considered.

performing A was not free. Thus, as many philosophers are attracted to the Principle of Alternate possibilities, they are likely to be reluctant to deny (7). I will sometimes refer to claim (7) as the Principle of Accidental Possibilities.

Some theists think there is a special motivation for endorsing the Principle of Alternate Possibilities, and so are likely to find that there is special reason for endorsing (7). This special reason derives from the fact that the Principle of Alternate Possibilities is thought (by these theists) to be part and parcel of an incompatibilist view of freedom, and an incompatibilist view of freedom is thought to provide the theist with a significant theoretical advantage in responding to what is widely regarded as the most important objection to theism—the problem of evil. Not only is it widely thought that Alvin Plantinga's (1974a) free will defense, which appeals explicitly to an incompatibilist account of freedom, successfully refuted the logical argument from evil,[10] but it is also widely thought that a successful theodicy for many specific evils will appeal to values possible only given an incompatibilist account of freedom.[11] Insofar, then, as an incompatibilist account of freedom provides the theist with such theoretical advantages and insofar as (7) is required for the defense of an incompatibilist view of freedom, the theist is significantly better off if she can affirm (7).

For purposes of this book I am most interested in dialoguing with theists attracted to the foregoing incompatibilist picture. As a result, I will tend to assume an incompatibilist account of freedom without argument. According to incompatibilist views, causal determinism and free will are incompatible. I will have much more to say about incompatibilism and causal determinism later. For now, I only wish to give the reader notice that my interest here will be in responses to the foreknowledge argument which are attractive from the perspective of incompatibilism. Thus, for example, when I discuss objections to (7) later, I will discuss only objections which have some chance of being endorsed by incompatibilists.

We are now ready to draw the final sub-conclusion of the foreknowledge argument:

(8) Elizabeth's singing a sonnet to John at t_{100} is not done freely.

Sub-conclusion (8) follows from (7) and (6). And, with (8), we are able to complete the conditional proof of the claim that *if* an infallible God forebelieved long ago that Elizabeth will sing John a love sonnet at t_{100}, then her doing so is not done freely. That is, we can now affirm, by conditional proof, that:

(9) If God believed at t_1 that Elizabeth would sing a love sonnet to John at t_{100} and if $\square_L$ $\forall t, t', S, A$ (God believes at t that S does A at t' $\rightarrow$ S does A at t'), then Elizabeth's singing a love sonnet to John at t_{100} is not done freely.

Since there was nothing special about Elizabeth and her sonnet, we can conclude that if an infallible God forebelieved long ago that *any* human agent will perform any action

---

[10] Though see Pruss (2012).
[11] See discussion in Tooley (2012).

at some future time, her doing so is not done freely. In other words, infallible divine foreknowledge is incompatible with human freedom. For ease of reference, I will repeat the foreknowledge argument in full here before moving on to consider parallel arguments for logical and causal fatalism.

The foreknowledge argument

(1) God believed at t_1 that Elizabeth would sing a love sonnet to John at t_{100}. (Supposition for Conditional Proof derived from divine cognitive perfection)

(2) $\Box_L \forall t, t', S, A$ (God believes at t that S does A at $t' \rightarrow$ S does A at t'). (Supposition for Conditional Proof derived from divine cognitive perfection)

(3) $\forall t, t', x [(x$ obtains at t and $t < t') \rightarrow (\Box_A$ at t' that x obtains at t)]. (Principle of the Necessity of the Past)

(4) $\Box_A$ at t_{100} that God believes at t_1 that Elizabeth will sing a love sonnet to John at t_{100}. (from (1) and (3))

(5) $\forall p, q, t [(\Box_A$ at t that p and $\Box_L (p \rightarrow q)) \rightarrow \Box_A$ at t that q]. (Transfer of Accidental Necessity principle)

(6) $\Box_A$ at t_{100} that Elizabeth sings a love sonnet to John at t_{100}. (from (2), (4), and (5))

(7) $\forall S, A, t (\Box_A$ at t that S does A at t $\rightarrow$ S's doing A at t is not done freely). (Principle of Alternate Accidental Possibilities)

(8) Elizabeth's singing a love sonnet to John at t_{100} is not done freely. (from (6) and (7))

(9) So, if God believed at t_1 that Elizabeth would sing a love sonnet to John at t_{100} and if $\Box_L \forall t, t', S, A$ (God believes at t that S does A at $t' \rightarrow$ S does A at t'), then Elizabeth's singing a love sonnet to John at t_{100} is not done freely. (from (1) and (2)–(8) by Conditional Proof)

2. The foreknowledge argument and the arguments for logical and causal fatalism

This section briefly presents two arguments which significantly parallel the foreknowledge argument presented in the previous section. I will call them *the argument for logical fatalism* and *the argument for causal fatalism*. Investigating these two arguments will help us develop standards for success in responses to the foreknowledge argument.

Begin with the argument for logical fatalism. Paralleling the informal argument presented earlier concerning freedom and foreknowledge, here is an informal presentation of the reasoning involved in the argument for logical fatalism:

There's nothing I can now do about whether some claim was true long ago. But, then, if it was true long ago that I will do certain things each day for the rest of my life, and if what was true cannot fail to be, then there's nothing I can now do about these things, either. So, if it was true long ago that I will do certain things each day for the rest of my life and if what was true cannot fail to be, then whether I do those things isn't up to me.

This informal line of reasoning is likely to strike a chord with those who have given much thought to the relationship between past truths about future actions and the nature of free action. But, at the same time, it is noteworthy that most readers will find this informal line of reasoning less powerful than the informal line of reasoning presented earlier concerning the relationship between freedom and divine foreknowledge.

Here is a formal version of the argument for logical fatalism—one which intentionally closely parallels the formal version of the foreknowledge argument made earlier:

The argument for logical fatalism

(1) It was true at t_1 that Elizabeth would sing a love sonnet to John at t_{100}. (Supposition for Conditional Proof)

(2) $\square_L \forall t, t', S, A$ (If it was true at t that S does A at $t' \rightarrow$ S does A at t'). (Premise)

(3) $\forall t, t', x$ [(x obtains at t and $t < t'$) $\rightarrow$ ($\square_A$ at t' that x obtains at t)). (Principle of the Necessity of the Past)

(4) $\square_A$ at t_{100} that it was true at t_1 that Elizabeth will sing a love sonnet to John at t_{100}. (from (1),(3))

(5) $\forall p, q, t$ [($\square_A$ at t that p and $\square_L (p \rightarrow q)) \rightarrow \square_A$ at t that q]. (Transfer of Accidental Necessity principle)

(6) $\square_A$ at t_{100} that Elizabeth sings a love sonnet to John at t_{100}. (from (2), (3) and (5))

(7) $\forall S, A, t$ ($\square_A$ at t that S does A at t $\rightarrow$ S's doing A at t is not done freely). (Principle of Accidental Possibilities)

(8) Elizabeth's singing a love sonnet to John at t_{100} is not done freely. (from (6) and (7))

(9) So, if it was true at t_1 that Elizabeth would sing a love sonnet to John at t_{100}, then Elizabeth's singing a love sonnet to John at t_{100} is not done freely. (from (1)–(8) by Conditional Proof)

The argument for logical fatalism selects an arbitrary future action, Elizabeth's singing a love sonnet to John, which is as good a candidate as any for a free action and it then attempts to show that if there is a proposition which reports her doing so which was true in the distant past, then her doing so is not done freely. Thus, for any agent and action at any time, if it was true long ago that this agent will perform this action at this time, her doing so is not done freely. The truth of propositions in the past undermines the existence of free action.

I will not here attempt a defense of the premises and inferences of the argument for logical fatalism which differ from those of the foreknowledge argument, as this will be discussed later. I only wish to note, again, that it has been quite common for philosophers to regard the argument for logical fatalism as less persuasive than the foreknowledge argument, whether or not they endorse the foreknowledge argument.[12] One lesson to take away from considering the argument for logical fatalism in

---

[12] See, e.g., Warfield (1997) and Zagzebski (2011).

comparison to the foreknowledge argument, then, is that a successful response to the foreknowledge argument should have something to say about this difference in the way these two very similar arguments are evaluated. Something must be said to either explain away or to accommodate the idea many have had that the foreknowledge argument is in some way more powerful than the argument for logical fatalism. This is a first success condition on responses to the foreknowledge argument.

Move now to the argument for causal fatalism. This argument attempts to show that if causal determinism is true, then an arbitrarily selected action of a human being which was just as good a candidate as any for a free action cannot be a free action. Thus, if causal determinism is true, there are no free actions. After representing the argument, I will comment more on what is meant by "causal determinism" and how this thesis makes its appearance in the argument as it is represented here.

An informal version of the argument for causal fatalism could be expressed as follows:

> If causal determinism is true, then whatever I do for the rest of my life is the consequence of the past and the laws of nature. But there's nothing I can now do about the past and the laws of nature. So, if causal determinism is true, there's nothing I can now do about what I do for the rest of my life, either. But, then, what I do the rest of my life isn't up to me.

The accompanying formal version is as follows:

The argument for causal fatalism

(1) The actual world was way W at t_1 and the laws of the actual world were L at t_1. (Supposition for Conditional Proof)

(2) $\Box_L$ (The actual world was way W at t_1 and the laws of the actual world were L at t_1 → Elizabeth sings a love sonnet to John at t_{100}). (Supposition for Conditional Proof)

(3) $\forall t, t', x$ [(x obtains at t and t < t') → ($\Box_A$ at t' that x obtains at t)]. (Principle of the Necessity of the Past)

(4) $\Box_A$ at t_{100} that the actual world was way W at t_1 and the laws of the actual world were L at t_1. (from (1) and (3))

(5) $\forall p, q, t$ [($\Box_A$ at t that p and $\Box_L(p{\to}q)$) → $\Box_A$ at t that q]. (Transfer of Accidental Necessity Principle)

(6) $\Box_A$ at t_{100} that Elizabeth sings a love sonnet to John at t_{100}. (from (2), (3) and (5))

(7) $\forall S, A, t$ ($\Box_A$ at t that S does A at t → S's doing A at t is not done freely). (Principle of Accidental Possibilities)

(8) Elizabeth's singing a love sonnet to John at t_{100} is not done freely. (from (6) and (7))

(9) So, [the actual world was way W at t_1 and the laws of the actual world were L at t_1 and $\Box_L$ (The actual world was way W at t_1 and the laws of the actual world were L at t_1 → Elizabeth sings a love sonnet to John at t_{100})] → Elizabeth's singing a love sonnet to John at t_{100} is not done freely. (from (1) and (2)–(8) by Conditional Proof)

The key differences between the argument for causal fatalism and the foreknowledge argument are to be found in claims (1) and (2). To understand (1) and (2) we must clarify what W and L are. First, W is a complete description of the state of the world at time t_1. The notion of a "way the world is" at a time is imprecise, but we needn't develop a more precise notion for present purposes. A lengthier discussion of what a "way the world is" at a time is offered in Chapter 4. Second, L is a complete conjunction of the laws of nature which govern the way things in the world operate at t_1. These laws are, presumably, the objects of scientific inquiry. Among them may be such laws as the laws of thermodynamics, for instance. Given these specifications of W and L, it is clear that (1) is assumed to be true by *definition* of W and L.

Claim (2) is the assumption in the argument where the thesis of causal determinism makes its appearance. Typically, causal determinism is formulated informally as the thesis that the past together with the laws of nature determine or fix the future. More formally, causal determinism is the thesis that for any times t and t′, if t is earlier than t′, then the way the world is at t′ is entailed by the conjunction of a complete description of the way the world was at t together with the laws of nature governing the world at t.[13] Symbolically, causal determinism states that $\forall$p, t, t′, x, W, L ([t < t′ and x obtains at t′ and the world is way W at t and the laws of the world are L at t] $\rightarrow \Box_L$ [(the world is way W at t and the laws of the world are L at t)$\rightarrow$ x obtains at t′]). In English, this says "that for every state of affairs x, time t and t′, way the world is W, and complete conjunction of laws L, if t is earlier than t′ and x obtains at t′ and the world is way W at t and the laws of the world are L at t, then it is logically necessary that if the world is way W at t and the laws of the world are L at t then x obtains at t′." Though a mouthful, the basic idea here is clear. It is logically impossible for the past and the laws to be as they in fact are and for the future to be different.

If the thesis of causal determinism is true, then claim (2) of the argument for causal fatalism is an innocent supposition. For, by (1), we are supposing that W and L characterize the actual world at t_1. And, it is a general supposition of the argument for causal fatalism that Elizabeth in fact does sing a love sonnet to John at t_{100}; this is simply the arbitrary action we have chosen to use in the argument. Thus, it follows, given causal determinism, that it is logically necessary that if the world is way W at t_1 and its laws are L at t_1 then Elizabeth sings her sonnet at t_{100}. And, this is just what (2) says. The remainder of the argument for causal fatalism trots along in exactly the same way as the foreknowledge argument and the argument for logical fatalism.

It is important to note here how closely the argument for causal fatalism parallels one of the most important arguments for incompatibilism about freedom and causal determinism—the consequence argument. There are slight variations in the presentations of the consequence argument and the argument for causal fatalism presented here. For example, as developed by Peter van Inwagen (1983), the consequence argument does not make use of accidental necessity, but rather a sort of necessity stipulatively defined by van Inwagen. Nonetheless, it is likely that those who

---

[13] See Hoefer (2010).

are attracted to the consequence argument will find the argument for causal fatalism attractive as well. Since, as I said before, I am especially interested in this book to dialogue with theists attracted to incompatibilist views of freedom, this parallelism is an important fact for us to keep in mind as we assess responses to the foreknowledge argument later. Other things being equal, a response to the foreknowledge argument which permits the success of either the argument for causal fatalism or an argument much like it will be preferable to a response that does not. This constitutes a second success condition on responses to the foreknowledge argument.

3. Responses to the foreknowledge argument

We should note one final, third success condition on responses to the foreknowledge argument before beginning to assess those which attack one of the argument's premises or inferences. For a response to the foreknowledge argument to be successful is not simply for it to show that there is something technically wrong with the foreknowledge argument as stated already. For, it could be that, even if the foreknowledge argument, as stated, does not succeed in showing that the motivations which it argues are in tension are indeed in tension, there may be an only slightly modified version of the foreknowledge argument that does succeed. Thus, the standard for success for responses to the foreknowledge argument must be to explain away this apparent tension between the motivations which the foreknowledge argument attempts to show are in tension with one another—the motivation on the one hand to affirm divine cognitive perfection and the motivation on the other hand to affirm significant freedom for human beings. Thus, we shall evaluate the responses to the foreknowledge argument later with a view toward determining not simply whether these responses show that the foreknowledge argument, as stated, fails, but whether these responses are able to show that the tension which the foreknowledge argument claims exists between the motivations for affirming divine cognitive perfection and significant human freedom in fact does not exist. One important consequence of this standard for success is that a response to the foreknowledge argument which exposes a technical flaw in the statement of the foreknowledge argument presented earlier may not be ultimately successful if this response does not rule out a slightly modified version of the foreknowledge argument.

With the foregoing three success conditions in place, it is time to turn to responses to the foreknowledge argument. Here I will investigate strategies which attempt to respond to the argument by denying one of its premises or inferences.

3.1 Rejections of (1) or (2)

I begin with several strategies which attempt to respond to the foreknowledge argument by denying one of its suppositions—either (1) or (2). At first glance, it may sound strange to call a reaction to the foreknowledge argument which denies one of its suppositions a "response" to that argument. For, to deny one of the suppositions of the argument is not to have shown that the argument itself does not succeed. It is simply to refuse to engage with the argument as stated.

Nevertheless, there may be some sense in calling at least some of the strategies I will momentarily discuss "responses" to the foreknowledge argument in light of what we said a moment ago about the standards for success in responses to the foreknowledge argument. For, while responses to the foreknowledge argument which deny its suppositions cannot and do not show that the foreknowledge argument as stated before fails, they may show that this argument shouldn't worry someone who is motivated by the two motivations which the foreknowledge argument attempts to show are in tension—the motivation to affirm divine cognitive perfection and the motivation to affirm significant human freedom. These responses will relieve such worries if they can show that the motivations which tend to lead one to affirm (1) and (2)—motivations which appeal to divine cognitive perfection—needn't lead one to affirm (1) and (2) and that the claims these motivations *do* lead one to adopt do not conflict with the motivation to affirm significant human freedom.

I'll begin with three strategies for denying the first supposition—the supposition that God believes at t_1 that Elizabeth sings a love sonnet to John at t_{100}. One strategy which rejects this supposition says that it is false because God doesn't have beliefs at all, much less this specific belief about Elizabeth. The standard motivations for claiming that God does have beliefs appeal to the role of beliefs in achieving cognitive goods like propositional knowledge—knowledge *that* such-and-such is the case. But, defenders of this strategy maintain that God could achieve comparable cognitive goods without beliefs, and so would not hold beliefs in addition to doing whatever is necessary for achieving these cognitive goods.[14] In fact, defenders of this strategy often think that believing that such-and-such is the case is an *inferior* way to achieve cognitive goods like knowledge. Perhaps this is because to achieve knowledge by believing that such-and-such is the case is to achieve knowledge in a piecemeal fashion as opposed to grasping the whole of reality at once,[15] or perhaps it is because to achieve knowledge in this way is to achieve knowledge only *indirectly* through propositional representations rather than through a direct apprehension of things themselves.[16] God's knowledge, by contrast, would be achieved through some kind of comprehensive intuitive perception or, if not, then through a direct awareness of each fact—but certainly not through beliefs.

The basic problem with this strategy is that, even if it succeeded in showing that the foreknowledge argument as stated is off-target, there is a simple modification which can be made to the foreknowledge argument which will result in an argument which is arguably just as powerful as the original. Rather than claiming in supposition (1) something about divine *belief*, the author of the argument ought to claim something about another relevant divine cognitive state. In particular, whatever psychological

---

[14] The classic paper here is Alston (1986).

[15] See, e.g., Aquinas *ST* Ia, Q14.

[16] This concern animates many defenders of the direct acquaintance account of knowledge, e.g., Price (1950).

state it is whereby God achieves his comprehensive intuitive vision or his direct acquaintance knowledge of Elizabeth's singing her sonnet to John at t_{100}—achievements the current strategy is happy to endorse—should be appealed to. Suppose, for example, that the psychological state whereby direct acquaintance is achieved is an awareness. Thus, (1) should be replaced by (1*): God had an awareness at t_1 as of Elizabeth's singing a love sonnet to John at t_{100}.[17] Of course, given God's cognitive perfection, it will be plausible that God's awarenesses cannot be misleading. Thus, we can replace (2) with (2*): $\Box_L$ ∀t, t′, S, A (God has an awareness at t as of S's doing A at t′ → S does A at t′). And the remainder of the foreknowledge argument will trot on as before. Thus, this response fails to relieve the tension the foreknowledge argument attempts to establish between the motivations for affirming divine cognitive perfection and significant human freedom.[18]

Move to a second way of denying (1). The approach denies (1) not because it denies that there are divine beliefs, but because it denies that there are divine beliefs *held at times*. This is because God is timeless.[19] Unfortunately, regardless of what other motivations there are for affirming divine timelessness, there are several reasons for thinking that it does not offer a successful response to the foreknowledge argument.

The first thing to notice about this response to the foreknowledge argument is that there is a parallel response that is sometimes offered against the argument for logical fatalism. Just as this response to the foreknowledge argument claims that God does not hold beliefs at times, some have responded to the argument for logical fatalism by claiming that propositions are not true at times.[20] And many of the same reasons which motivate people to deny that God is in time also motivate people to deny that propositions are in time. This observation makes trouble for the timelessness solution because, as we said before, a successful response to the foreknowledge argument ought to make it clear why this argument is thought to have theoretical advantages over the argument for logical fatalism.

The difficulties for the timelessness strategy get only more serious. Suppose we grant that it is possible that God is outside of time but infallibly, timelessly believes that Elizabeth sings her sonnet to John at t_{100}. Several philosophers have argued that this possibility will imply the possibility of there being temporal correlates of these divine timeless beliefs. Such temporal correlates might include prophetic utterances, divinely inscribed monuments, or even the beliefs of an incarnate God.[21] Thus, only slightly modified versions of the foreknowledge argument, versions which use these temporal

---

[17] It is noteworthy here that an awareness *as of* x is plausibly thought of as the purely psychological component of an awareness *of* x.

[18] The strategy might be revived if there are mental states whereby God achieves infallible foreknowledge of future creaturely acts which do not themselves entail the occurrence of these acts. See notes 26 and 27.

[19] See, e.g., Boethius *The Consolation of Philosophy* for a classic source and Stump and Kretzmann (1981) and Rota (2010) for contemporary sources. Craig (2009) offers a critical overview of the position and its rivals.

[20] See Ayer (1963) and van Inwagen (1983).

[21] See van Inwagen (2008) and Zagzebski (2012).

correlates of divine beliefs, will be possible. So the timelessness solution will not have provided us with a successful response to the foreknowledge argument.

Finally, and perhaps most importantly, even if we were not troubled by arguments involving the potential temporal correlates of divine beliefs just discussed, some philosophers have argued that we should still be worried by an only slightly modified version of the foreknowledge argument—this one focused on the timeless beliefs themselves. Linda Zagzebski (2012) has suggested that, in the face of the timelessness solution, the advocate of the foreknowledge argument ought to replace the suppositions of the foreknowledge argument as follows. Supposition (1) should be replaced by (1*): God *timelessly* believes that Elizabeth sings a love sonnet to John at t_{100}. And, supposition (2) should be replaced by (2*): $\Box_L$ $\forall t, t', S, A$ (God timelessly believes that S does A at $t' \to$ S does A at t'). In order for the modified argument to trot on as before, one more modification will be needed, however. The Principle of the Necessity of the Past must be replaced by a Principle of the Necessity of the Timeless. Instead of

(3) $\forall t, t', x$ [(x obtains at t and $t < t'$) $\to$ ($\Box_A$ at t' that x obtains at t)). (Principle of the Necessity of the Past)

we will have

(3*) $\forall t, x$ [(x obtains timelessly) $\to$ ($\Box_A$ at t that x obtains timelessly)). (Principle of the Necessity of the Timeless)

With (3*) in hand, the remainder of the argument will trot on as before. In order to respond to the resulting modified timeless knowledge argument and thereby have a successful response to the foreknowledge argument, the advocate of timelessness must reject either (1*), (2*), or (3*). However, the doctrine of divine timelessness itself does not threaten any of these claims. So, something in addition to this doctrine is needed for a successful response to the foreknowledge argument, given our standards for success presented earlier. Unfortunately, the kinds of candidates for this something else that have been brought forward by advocates of the timelessness solution are considerations which would threaten the original foreknowledge argument just as much as the modified timeless knowledge argument; and they would do so quite independently of the doctrine of timelessness. For example, Michael Rota (2010) argues against (3*) on the basis of a metaphor according to which divine timeless "seeing" is explanatorily posterior to human free action. But, Rota does not argue that this idea about divine "seeing" couldn't be adopted just as well by those who think God is temporal. He doesn't show, that is, that they couldn't claim that God's "seeing" in the past the future actions of human beings is explanatorily posterior to those future actions, and so (3) is false. Accordingly, if the considerations Rota brings forward threaten (3*), then those considerations threaten (3) just as well, and they do so independently of timelessness. The doctrine of timelessness plays no essential role in a successful response to the foreknowledge argument. The success of the timelessness solution stands or falls with the success of other proposed solutions; so, our attention should turn to those.

One final strategy for denying supposition (1) denies it not because God holds no beliefs and not because God holds no beliefs at times, but because God holds no beliefs *about the future actions of free creatures* at times. Someone who advocates this strategy will want to explain *why* God doesn't hold any beliefs about these matters in a way that does not threaten divine cognitive perfection. Here I know of two suggestions, each of which is a version of open theism.

The first open theist explanation for why God doesn't hold beliefs about the future actions of creatures is that God only believes what is true, and there are no truths about what these creatures will do. At least, there are no truths about what these creatures will do when what they do is done *freely*. Thus, for any action A and any creature S, if time t is earlier than time t′ and S is free with respect to doing A or not-A at t′, then at t God will not hold a belief about whether or not S does A at t′, since neither the claim that S does A at t′ nor the claim that S does not do A at t′ is true at t. Of course, there are two ways to hold that a claim is not true. One may hold that the claim is not true because it is false or because it has no truth-value. Thus, there are two options for open theists here. They may affirm that God won't believe claims about the future free actions of creatures either because these claims are all false,[22] or because they have no truth value.[23] Advocates of this strategy have suggested that their view does no real damage to divine cognitive perfection. For, they can maintain a straightforward and attractive account of divine omniscience according to which for all propositions p, necessarily, if p is true then God knows p and if God believes p then p is true.

I will highlight two difficulties for this strategy. First, this strategy does not offer a successful response to the foreknowledge argument by itself, because it puts the foreknowledge argument on par with the argument for logical fatalism. Both arguments fail for precisely the same reason, according to this solution—propositions about what creatures will freely do are not true in the past. But, as we saw earlier, a successful response to the foreknowledge argument ought to explain why the foreknowledge argument has been taken to pose a more significant threat to freedom than that posed by the argument for logical fatalism.

Second, these versions of open theism require embracing a highly questionable semantics for future- and past-tensed sentences. As Alan Rhoda has made clear, "what underlies these positions is a (usually tacit) commitment to what Prior has dubbed the 'Peircean' system of tense logic and opposed to the more common 'Ockhamist' system.... Peirceans hold that the grounding for *all* truths lies in the present" (2008: 230). Thus, Rhoda explains that "whether a proposition about the future is true *at a given time* depends on whether sufficient conditions for its truth obtain at that time" (2007: 306). Similarly, we might infer that whether a proposition about the past is true at a given time depends on whether sufficient conditions for its truth obtain at that time. By "sufficient conditions," Rhoda makes it clear that he means *causally* sufficient conditions.

[22] As in Rhoda, Boyd, and Belt (2006).
[23] As in Lucas (1989).

This Peircean semantics is vulnerable to several powerful objections. First, as Fredosso (1988) has stressed, it has difficulty accounting for our common practices of retroactively describing statements about future contingents as true simply because matters later turned out as the statements said they would. For example, we might imagine someone who predicts of a coin flip he knows to be indeterministic that "it will land heads." If it turns out that the coin does land heads, it would not be strange at all to claim that the speaker was correct; but, the Peircean cannot permit this since causally sufficient conditions for the coin's landing heads were not in place.[24]

And matters only get worse. Imagine you are the flipper of the indeterministic coin. And, imagine that you are in as good a position as one can be with respect to determining that there are not causally sufficient conditions in place for the coin's landing one way or another. The claim that the coin lands heads in the near future is incredibly unlikely for you, given a Peircean semantics. So long as you retain your confidence that the coin-flipping is an indeterministic process, your confidence level should remain extremely low that the coin soon lands heads. But this commitment has unacceptable results. Just imagine that before you flip, your reliable time-traveling friend enters the room and tells you sincerely that he has just returned from the near future having observed your coin landing heads. If the Peircean semantics is correct and there is no adjustment in your confidence that the coin-flipping is an indeterministic process, then it would be irrational for you to adjust your confidence in the claim that the coin soon lands heads in light of your friend's report. But surely this is incorrect—you very well ought to adjust your confidence in the claim that the coin will land heads even if you retain the view that the flip is indeterministic.[25] A parallel objection may be run with respect to past truths for which there are not presently causally sufficient conditions.[26]

The second variety of open theism maintains that God does not hold beliefs about the future free actions of creatures in the past not because there is no truth of the matter concerning these claims, but because the claims cannot be known—not by God or by anyone else. According to this view, it may well be true at t_1 that Elizabeth will sing a love sonnet to John at t_{100}, but this truth is not one which is knowable by anyone at times prior to t_{100}. Thus, God will not believe it at t_1.[27]

At first glance, it may seem quite straightforward how we are to understand the view of omniscience advocated by defenders of this third strategy. We should say, simply, that

---

[24] See Rhoda (2007) for a reply.

[25] The example does not require the possibility of time travel, since it can be run using the (if time travel is impossible) counterpossible conditional: *were one to receive such a report for a reliable time traveling friend, one's confidence in the relevant future-tensed claim should not be adjusted.* For more on using counterpossible conditionals in this way see Merricks (2001), Vander Laan (2004), and Berto (2009).

[26] Advocates of the present strategy might reply, as Rhoda (2010) does to Pruss (2010), that what is likely is only that <the coin lands (non-temporally) heads> will soon *become* true. But this strategy is unmotivated in the absence of a prior commitment to the Peircean semantics and it leaves the advocate of the present strategy vulnerable to a modified foreknowledge argument which replaces (1) with (1*): God believes at t_1 that <Elizabeth sings to John> is true at t_{100}.

[27] For defenses of this view, see Hasker (1989) and van Inwagen (2008).

(LFOT1) God is omniscient = $\forall$p, t [(p is true at t and $\Diamond_L$ (Someone knows p at t))
$\rightarrow$ God knows p at t]

In English, the view says that "for God to be omniscient is just for it to be the case that for every proposition p and time t, if p is true at t and it is logically possible for someone to know p at t then God knows p at t." However, the lesson of one important objection to this strategy seems to be that this definition of omniscience is not careful enough.

Alexander Pruss (2011) argues that, given rather trivial assumptions, it follows that if God satisfies LFOT1's analysis of omniscience, then God must know all truths *simpliciter*—not just all knowable truths. Suppose, for illustration, that it is true that at t_{100} Elizabeth sings her sonnet to John. Now, select an arbitrary contingently true proposition q such that it is logically possible for someone to know q at t_1 and also logically possible at t_1 that someone knows not-q. Now, it will follow from LFOT1 that God knows q, since q is true and it is logically possible for someone to know q. But, it will also follow from LFOT1, argues Pruss, that God knows the proposition <either not-q or Elizabeth sings her sonnet to John at t_{100}>, since this proposition is true and there is a possible world where God knows it, given that there is a possible world where God knows not-q. But now, since God's knowledge is closed under strict implication, and God knows both <either not-q or Elizabeth sings her sonnet to John at t_{100}> and q, God must also know that Elizabeth sings her sonnet to John at t_{100}. The same proof can be repeated for God's knowledge of other claims about what creatures do in the future.

A key principle relied upon in Pruss's argument is that if a proposition p is known by someone at time t in a possible world w, then p is knowable at t. This claim is correct so long as knowability is explained using logical possibilities as in LFOT1. But, there are other ways that knowability might be explained. For example, it might be explained using *ways* of knowing, as in LFOT2:

(LFOT2) God is omniscient = $\forall$p, t [(p is true at t and there is a way to know p at t)
$\rightarrow$ God knows p at t]

According to LFOT2, God's omniscience consists in its being the case that for all propositions p and times t, if p is true at t and *there is a way* to know p at t, then God knows p at t. The advocate of this account of divine omniscience might maintain that the fact that a proposition is known at a time in a possible world is not sufficient for it to be the case that there is a way to know that proposition at that time in the actual world. This idea has some plausibility, since it is plausible returning to Pruss's specific case that the way whereby God knows <either not-q or Elizabeth sings her sonnet to John at t_{100}> in a possible world in his example—by God knowing not-q and using deduction—is not a way of knowing this claim in the actual world. After all, not-q is not *true* in the actual world. Thus, LFOT2 remains faithful to the central idea behind the present strategy, and it is not vulnerable to Pruss's objection.

What this defense of the present strategy brings out is that it is central to the present strategy that there is no *way* for God or anyone else to know infallibly at least some propositions reporting the future free actions of creatures. Accordingly, if we do not know that there is no way to know infallibly the future free actions of creatures, then we will not be in a position to know that the present strategy is a success. Since it is a primary aim of the present book to show that we do not know that there are no ways for God to know infallibly what free creatures will do, I will not discuss the present strategy any further here.

This concludes our discussion of strategies which respond to the foreknowledge argument by denying its first supposition. There are, in addition, two strategies which respond to the foreknowledge argument by denying its *second* supposition—the claim that, necessarily, for all agents S, actions A, and times t and t', if God believes at t that S does A at t', then S does A at t'. As we saw earlier, this premise is supposed to be supported by God's cognitive perfection, specifically by the claim that God does not and cannot make cognitive mistakes. Thus, strategies which reject this claim, if they are to be successful in the sense explained earlier, must explain how it is possible to deny this claim and yet maintain God's cognitive perfection.

One important strategy which does just this has recently been revived by Patrick Todd (2011). The view, which Todd calls "Geachianism" after the philosopher Peter Geach,[28] shares in common with other views we have discussed the idea that propositions change their truth-values. In particular, Geachianism maintains that it can be that a proposition such as <Elizabeth will sing a love sonnet to John at t_{100}> can be true at one time t prior to t_{100} and not true at another time t'. Thus, it could be that God believes at t_1 that Elizabeth will sing a love sonnet to John at t_{100} and that God is correct, since at t_1 it is true that Elizabeth will sing a love sonnet to John at t_{100}, yet it does not follow from this that Elizabeth will sing a love sonnet to John at t_{100}. Rather, it only follows from this that *at* t_1 Elizabeth will sing a love sonnet to John at t_{100}. Thus, the second supposition in the foreknowledge argument is false. But it is false in a way that appears consistent with divine cognitive perfection, since the Geachian can maintain that God never holds any belief at any time where the belief held is not true at that time.

The primary motivation offered for Geachianism is that Geachianism is thought to provide a more promising account of prevention than those accounts provided by non-Geachian views. According to the Geachian, what is prevented is what was going to happen but didn't happen. Yet, if anything was going to happen and didn't happen, then plausibly it was true at some time that something was going to happen and then later no longer true that this was going to happen. Todd has claimed that this can happen in the case of free actions of creatures. At some past times it was going to be the case that a free creature behaves one way, but at later past times this was no longer the case.

Unfortunately, Geachianism suffers from two very serious difficulties.[29] First, it has been argued that the Geachian analysis of prevention is not superior to non-Geachian analyses. The kinds of cases typically thought to support Geachianism over

---

[28] See Geach (1977).
[29] See fuller discussion in (Byerly 2012a).

non-Geachian views are cases where the prevention of an event is overdetermined. The best non-Geachian account of prevention, it has been argued, is an account according to which that which is prevented is what *would* have happened but didn't. But, in cases of overdetermination, the prevented event isn't something that *would* have happened. The problem with this argument is that there is a better non-Geachian account of prevention which handles cases of overdetermination adequately. According to this superior non-Geachian account, that which is prevented is that the non-occurrence of which is explained. Events the non-occurrence of which is overdetermined are events the non-occurrence of which is explained; so, there is no trouble for this non-Geachain account of prevention in such cases.

Moreover, the explanation-based, non-Geachian account of prevention has a significant advantage over the Geachian account. The Geachian account implies that in cases of indeterministic processes, if one indeterministic outcome was going to happen but didn't, then it was prevented from happening. Yet, this seems incorrect. The explanation-based, non-Geachian account needn't imply that such indeterministic processes are prevented, since their non-occurrence may not have a sufficient explanation. If anything, the Geachian view of prevention seems *worse* off than its rivals.

Even more importantly in our present context, the Geachian view cannot plausibly be used in the way Todd wishes to explain how supposition two in the foreknowledge argument could fail. For, the mechanism whereby the Geachian proposes that propositions change their truth-value is the mechanism of prevention. Thus, if we had a case where the Geachian wants to claim that at one time it was going to be the case that Elizabeth sings a love sonnet to John at t_{100}, but at later times this was no longer the case, the Geachian will be claiming that this is so because Elizabeth's singing her sonnet at t_{100} is *prevented*. But, plausibly, if Elizabeth's singing is *prevented*, then whether she sings is *not up to her*. Thus, the Geachian will not be able to maintain both the commitment to free action and the commitment to divine cognitive perfection which are required for a successful response to the foreknowledge argument.

A second approach which denies supposition two is one which claims that while God has exhaustive knowledge of the future, including knowledge of what creatures will freely do, God does not have *infallible* knowledge of these claims. God *could* be wrong, claims the advocate of this strategy, but God, in fact, never *is* wrong. And, the fact that God could be wrong is no problem for divine cognitive perfection. For, one of the lessons of the literature on the Gettier problem is that there can be cases where two subjects perform equally well as epistemic agents, but one could have (easily) been wrong and the other couldn't have (easily) been.[30] Thus, while God could have been wrong in some of his beliefs, this will not threaten the value of his epistemic performance.

Unfortunately for this strategy, it is difficult to defend the claim that while God could have been wrong in some of his beliefs, he never in fact is wrong in any of

---

[30] See Kvanvig (2003).

them. This is because of the problem of dwindling probabilities.[31] What this problem highlights is that when the likelihood of a claim p depends upon the likelihoods of other claims q and r, and neither q nor r is epistemically certain, the likelihood of p is less than the likelihood of each of q and r. Thus, if the epistemic likelihood of any claim p depends, for God, on the epistemic likelihood of other claims q and r, then if q and r are not epistemically certain, the likelihood of p will dwindle in comparison. The problem gets worse if there are chains of likelihoods—if, that is, the likelihood of q depends upon the likelihood of r, which depends upon the likelihood of s, and so on. Thus, if God could have been wrong in his beliefs, and if his belief structure contains chains of likelihoods, then there are some claims God does not in fact know.[32] In order to maintain her position coherently, the advocate of the present strategy must find a response to this problem of dwindling probabilities.

3.2 Rejections of (3): The necessity of the past

We can now move on to responses to the foreknowledge argument which do not deny one of its suppositions, but instead deny one of its premises or inferences. We will move premise by premise, evaluating first those responses which deny claim (3) of the argument—the Principle of the Necessity of the Past. Advocates of this response maintain that it is not the case that for all t, t′, and x, if x obtains at t and t is earlier than t′, then that x obtained at t is accidentally necessary at t′. Often, such thinkers are called "Ockhamists," though it is important to notice that this label is inexact.

There are at least two reasons one might opt for Ockhamism and deny (3). First, one might dispute (3) because one thinks that there are special cases where something obtained in the past such that it is not now necessary (i.e., not *accidentally* necessary) that it obtained. Perhaps most of what obtained in the past is now necessary, but some special cases of things which occurred in the past are not now necessary. There is an important difference, on this view, between what might be called "hard" features of the past—the obtaining of which *is* now necessary—and "soft" features of the past—the obtaining of which is *not* now necessary.[33]

What kinds of features might be soft features of the past? One suggestion is that the being true of propositions about the future fits in this category. For example, supposing that Elizabeth sings to John at t_{100}, let us grant that the proposition <Elizabeth sings to John at t_{100}> was true at t_1. Arguably, the being true of this proposition is something that obtained at t_1. But, also arguably, that Elizabeth sings to John at t_{100} is not something which is necessary at times later than t_1 and earlier than t_{100}. At times between t_1 and t_{100}, it is not impossible that Elizabeth *not* sing to John at t_{100}. And if at some such time it is possible that Elizabeth not sing to John at t_{100}, then it is not true that if x obtained at t and t is earlier than t′, then it is accidentally necessary at t′ that x obtained at t.

---

[31] The problem is discussed in general and applied to natural theology in particular in (Plantinga 2000: 270–80). For discussion, see Swinburne (2004), McGrew (2006), Plantinga (2006) and McGrew and McGrew (2008).

[32] See further Borland (2006).

[33] For a helpful introduction to the hard/soft distinction, see Todd (2013).

Another example. Suppose that at t_1 an asteroid is whizzing by the earth. And again suppose that Elizabeth sings to John at t_{100}. Thus, an asteroid whizzed by ninety-nine times (i.e., ninety-nine temporal units) before Elizabeth would sing to John. Arguably, an asteroid's whizzing by ninety-nine times before Elizabeth sings to John obtained at t_1. But, also arguably, that an asteroid whizzed by ninety-nine times before Elizabeth sings to John is not something which, at times between t_1 and t_{100}, is necessary. At times between t_1 and t_{100} it arguably remains possible that it is not the case that an asteroid whizzed by ninety-nine times before Elizabeth sings to John.

There are two hurdles facing those who advocate this strategy of denying (3). First, some will find it questionable whether the truth of propositions about the future and the whizzing by of asteroids many times before the occurrence of other events are things which really do *obtain* in the past. Indeed, some have emphasized this very fact in their response to the foreknowledge argument, as we will see in more detail later. But, if these things did *not* obtain in the past, then they and similar examples cannot be used to challenge the Principle of the Necessity of the Past.

The second hurdle for the present approach to denying (3) is that its advocate must not only show that (3) fails, but that divine beliefs about the future free actions of creatures held at times are among the special, soft features of the past rather than among the ordinary, hard features of the past. The approach many philosophers have taken here has been to define what soft features of the past are and to argue that past divine beliefs satisfy this account of softness.[34] However, one of the key lessons of the literature on soft and hard features of the past is that it is notoriously difficult to define soft and hard features of the past in such a way that, first, it is clear that past divine beliefs about the future free actions of creatures qualify as soft and, second, other features of the past that seem not to be soft clearly do not qualify as soft.[35]

A second approach to denying (3) is to deny it because one simply does not think there is any such thing as accidental necessity.[36] Again, I see two hurdles this strategy faces.

First, an advocate of this strategy must explain away the data which has motivated philosophers to maintain that there is such a thing as accidental necessity. For example, she must explain without appealing to accidental necessity why we are strongly inclined to grant that it was possible for Lincoln not to be shot prior to his being shot but that, now, after the shooting, it is no longer possible that Lincoln not be shot.

Perhaps the most promising approach here is to resort to the notion of causability— that which is causable. The reason we are inclined to say that it is possible that Lincoln not be shot prior to his shooting but not afterward is that, his not being shot is causable prior to the shooting but not afterward. Thus, the advocate of the present strategy would be suggesting that, while (3) is false, another claim much like it is true. Namely, (3*): for all x, t and t', if x obtains at t and t is earlier than t', then x's obtaining at t is

---

[34] See, e.g., Saunders (1966), Adams (1967), Fredosso (1983), Hoffman and Rosenkrantz (1984), Plantinga (1986), and Fischer, Todd, and Tognazini (2009).

[35] See especially Fischer (1992), Fischer, Todd, and Tognazini (2009) and Todd (2013).

[36] Both (Merricks 2009) and (Zagzebski 2011) express sympathy for this position.

uncausable at t'. Claim (3*) is supposed to be accounting for the data which tends to lead philosophers to endorse the necessity of the past.

Without further supplementation, the present strategy does not offer a successful response to the foreknowledge argument, however. For, an only slightly modified version of that argument can now be constructed which uses (3*) rather than (3).[37] The modified argument will employ a removal of Causabilities principle as opposed to a transfer of Accidental Necessity principle and a Principle of Alternate Causabilities, rather than a Principle of Alternate (Accidental) Possibilities. Thus, if we use $\square_C$ to symbolize "it is uncausable that," then instead of (5), the transfer of Accidental Necessities principle, we will have something like (5*): $\forall x, t, t'$ [(x obtains at t and $\square_C$ at t' (x obtains at t) and $\square_L$(x obtains at t $\rightarrow$ p)) $\rightarrow$ $\square_C$ at t' ($\sim$p)]. According to (5*), if something x obtains which is uncausable at a time t, and x's obtaining entails that something else y obtains, then no alternative to y is causable at t. Instead of (7), the Principle of Accidental Possibilities, we will have a Principle of Alternate Causabilities much like (7*): $\forall S, A, t$ ($\square_C$ at t (S does other than A) $\rightarrow$ S does not do A freely at t). (7*) tells us that in order for S to freely perform an action A at a time t, it must be that S's doing other than A is causable at t. The remainder of the foreknowledge argument will trot on as before.

The modified version of the foreknowledge argument is especially troubling for advocates of the present strategy who wish to uphold the basic idea behind the argument for causal fatalism—something we said was required for a successful response to the foreknowledge argument. The reason for this is that such a person will think, following the argument for causal fatalism, that if future events are the entailed consequences of past events, then this removes alternatives which are necessary for free action. But, given her advocacy of the present strategy, she denies that these alternatives are alternative accidental possibilities. A natural substitute is that they are alternative causabilities. Thus, such a person will think that if events obtain in the past which are presently uncausable and which entail the occurrence of other events, then alternatives to the latter events will be uncausable now. And, she will think that if alternatives to what will occur are all uncausable, then what will occur is not up to anyone in the sense required for free action. But these are the very two claims necessary for making the modified version of the foreknowledge argument presented here succeed. So, it would appear based on the present strategy that the argument for causal fatalism stands or falls with the foreknowledge argument.

The second hurdle for someone who denies (3) by claiming that there is no such thing as accidental necessity is similar to the point just discussed. The hurdle is created by the fact that not only the foreknowledge argument but the arguments for logical and causal fatalism presented earlier make use of the notion of accidental necessity. Thus, if there is no such thing as accidental necessity, then each of those arguments is threatened equally. But, it is problematic for a response to the foreknowledge argument to threaten the arguments for logical and causal fatalism just as much as the foreknowledge argument, as we emphasized before. The present strategy, then, suffers

---

[37] For further elaboration of this objection, see (Byerly forthcoming).

both in that there are slightly modified versions of the foreknowledge argument it does not rule out and in that it appears to threaten the arguments for causal and logical fatalism just as much as the foreknowledge argument.

3.3 Ockhamism 2.0: Denying the inference of (4) from (1) and (3)

Claim (4) in the foreknowledge argument says that it is accidentally necessary at t_{100} that God believed at t_1 that Elizabeth will sing a love sonnet to John at t_{100}. This claim is supposed to follow from claims (1) and (3). But, claim (4) does not follow from claims (1) and (3) without an additional posit which might be denied.

Recall that claim (1) is the supposition that God believes at t_1 that Elizabeth will sing a love sonnet to John at t_{100} and that claim (3) is that for all x, t and t', if x obtained at t and t is earlier than t', then it is accidentally necessary at t' that x obtained at t. If (4) is to follow from (1) and (3), the additional posit that God's believing that Elizabeth will sing a love sonnet to John at t_{100} is something that *obtained* at t_1. Some thinkers whose views are typically called "Ockhamist" might prefer this option to the option of denying claim (3) in one of the ways discussed in the previous subsection.[38]

Why would someone *not* think that God's believing that Elizabeth will sing a love sonnet to John at t_{100} is something that obtained at t_1? Perhaps for reasons quite similar to those discussed earlier for why someone might think that past divine beliefs about the future free actions of creatures belong to a group of special counterexamples to the Principle of the Necessity of the Past. One might argue that certain things which it is tempting to describe as having obtained in the past did not in fact obtain in the past. For example, the being true of the proposition <Elizabeth sings to John at t_{100}> is something which is tempting to describe as having obtained in the past. The advocate of the present strategy may even grant that this proposition was true at past times. But she will deny that the being true of this proposition *obtained* in the past. Rather, the proposition's being true either obtained at no time or it obtained partly in the past and partly not in the past.

Similarly, one might maintain that an asteroid's whizzing by ninety-nine temporal units before Elizabeth sings to John is something that did not obtain in the past, but something which either obtained at no time or obtained partly in the past and partly not in the past. This may be so even if it is true that an asteroid whizzed by ninety-nine temporal units prior to Elizabeth's singing.

Someone pursuing the present iteration of Ockhamism will likewise maintain that while it is tempting to describe divine beliefs about the future free actions of creatures as having obtained in the past, and while it is even true that God held these beliefs at past times, it is not the case that God's holding these beliefs is something that *obtained*

---

[38] See, e.g., the "Ockhamist" view discussed in (Warfield 2010) and criticized in (Byerly 2011). More speculatively, it may be that Zemach and Widerker's (1987) wide content construal of divine beliefs and Zagzebski's (1996) Thomistic Ockhamist view are most charitably interpreted as taking this approach to the foreknowledge argument rather than an approach which denies (3).

in the past. Although there is more to be said here,[39] the basic difficulty for this response to the foreknowledge argument is that so long as it is granted with (1) that divine beliefs about the future free actions of creatures were held in the past, it is very difficult to see how it could be denied that these divine beliefs obtained in the past. Beliefs held at past times, whether divine or not, seem to be among the clearest examples one could imagine of genuine features of the past.[40] They do not at all seem to be things which partly obtained in the past and partly did not obtain in the past or things which never obtained. The present strategy, then, faces a steep uphill climb.[41]

3.4 Denying the transfer of accidental necessity principle

Only a few writers have proposed denying the transfer of Accidental Necessity principle, claim (5) in the foreknowledge argument.[42] According to this principle, if p is accidentally necessary at t and p entails q, then q is accidentally necessary at t.[43] As we saw before, the principle is typically supported by the fact that transfer principles after which it is modeled are widely thought to hold for other kinds of necessity, such as logical necessity. Those who have proposed denying the transfer of Accidental Necessity principle have consequently tended to stress the difference between accidental necessity, whatever it is, and those kinds of necessity for which transfer principles are clearly correct.

Probably the most promising strategy here is akin to one we discussed earlier concerning the relationship between accidental necessity and causability. The approach here would be to simply define accidental necessity in terms of causability. Thus, for p to be accidentally necessary is for what p reports to be uncausable, and for p to be accidentally possible is for what p reports to be causable. The transfer principle in the foreknowledge argument would therefore be claiming that if what p reports is uncausable and p entails q, then what q reports is uncausable. It has been shown that this principle is false.[44]

---

[39] For example, if we understand Zagzebski (1996) and Zemach and Widerker (1987) in the way suggested in the previous footnote, then we get an initially plausible story about how the central claim here could be maintained. What makes it true that God believed that Elizabeth will sing is not that a belief state with this content obtained in the past, but that some state in the divine mind with an as-of-yet unspecified content obtained. One difficulty which such views must address is the difficulty of explaining how one and the same state in the divine mind with as-of-yet unspecified content could explain dramatically different divine behaviors in different possible worlds.

[40] Zagzebski (2011) is emphatic about this point.

[41] Fredosso (1988) has argued additionally that Ockhamist positions of the sort discussed here do not provide successful responses to the foreknowledge argument since slightly modified foreknowledge arguments can be developed where the subject is not divine beliefs but something which very clearly did obtain in the past, such as prophetic utterances.

[42] See Zagzebski (2011) and Byerly (2011).

[43] It is important to emphasize this way of stating the transfer principle as a principle according to which p *logically entails* q. Transfer principles which do not make use of logical entailment have been challenged (see McKay and Johnston 1996), but principles like the present one have been defended against the objections offered to their look-alikes (see Finch and Warfield 1998).

[44] Zagzebski (2011).

Despite the fact that the transfer of Accidental Necessity principle is false if accidental necessity is understood as uncausability, the present response to the foreknowledge argument faces the same difficulty highlighted earlier for the response to the foreknowledge argument which denies the necessity of the past on the basis that there is no such thing as accidental necessity. Namely, an only slightly modified version of the foreknowledge argument can be presented which, instead of the transfer of Accidental Necessity principle, invokes a removal of Accidental Possibilities principle, such as (5*): $\forall$x, t, t′ [(x obtains at t and $\Box_A$ at t′ (x obtains at t) and $\Box_L$ (x obtains at t → p)) → ~$\Diamond_A$ at t′ (~p)]. Where accidental necessity is defined in terms of causability, (5*) implies that if x obtains at t and x's obtaining at t is uncausable at t′, then if x's obtaining at t entails that y obtains at t′, no alternative to y's obtaining at t′ is causable at t′. Replacing (5) with (5*) will permit the foreknowledge argument to trot on as before, and (5*) is likely to be found plausible by those who would advocate the present strategy while seeking to maintain the basic idea behind the argument for causal fatalism.

There is a second, related difficulty for anyone who wishes to escape the foreknowledge argument by denying the transfer of Accidental Necessity principle. The difficulty is created by the fact that not only the foreknowledge argument but the arguments for logical and causal fatalism presented earlier make use of the transfer of Accidental Necessity principle. Thus, if this principle fails, then each of those arguments is threatened equally.

3.5 Denying the principle of alternate accidental possibilities

A final response to the foreknowledge argument involves denying claim (7), the Principle of Alternate Accidental Possibilities. According to this claim, in order for S to do A freely, it must not be the case that S's doing A is accidentally necessary.

We saw earlier that one of the central reasons for affirming (7) derives from the fact that (7) is simply a special instance of the Principle of Alternate Possibilities (PAP), which has been widely endorsed. Indeed, Kevin Timpe (2006b) claims that prior to 1969 both compatibilists and incompatibilists about freedom and causal determinism endorsed some version of PAP.

But things did change in 1969 when Harry Frankfurt (1969) presented his famous counterfactual intervener counterexample to PAP. Since 1969, numerous adaptations of Frankfurt's basic scenario have appeared in the literature.[45] What is essential to such cases is that an agent S performs some act A of S's own volition, but there is a mechanism in place to ensure that if S does not do A of S's own volition, the mechanism itself will ensure that S nonetheless does A. Frankfurt and others following him have thought that such cases show that PAP is false. They claim that in these scenarios, the agent S is morally responsible and free in performing action A even though S couldn't have done otherwise.

Several leading defenders of these Frankfurt examples are compatibilists about freedom and causal determinism who claim that the success of these examples is a

---

[45] See McKenna and Widerker (2006).

dialectical advantage to the compatibilist.[46] But, there have also been some prominent incompatibilists about freedom and causal determinism who have defended the examples.[47] Running somewhat against the grain of more typical incompatibilists,[48] they claim that while freedom requires the absence of causal determinism, it doesn't require the presence of alternate possibilities. It is this latter crowd which is especially relevant here, as I made clear before that my primary target audience is those theists who are attracted to incompatibilist accounts of freedom.

Accordingly, we must ask whether it is reasonable to deny (7) in the foreknowledge argument on the basis of Frankfurt-like scenarios while still retaining incompatibilism. I see two reasons for skepticism. The first reason comes from the fact that the argument for causal fatalism relies upon the Principle of Alternate Accidental Possibilities just as well as the foreknowledge argument. Thus, if this principle is false, both arguments will fail equally. At the very least, an incompatibilist who advocates denying (7) must find some alternate way of supporting her incompatibilism if she is to maintain that her doing so is as reasonable as it might have been if she had found an alternate way out of the foreknowledge argument.[49]

The second reason for skepticism is that there is powerful reason to think that an incompatibilist should not be moved by Frankfurt-like scenarios to deny PAP. At least, she should not be moved by them to deny every version of PAP which is relevant to the foreknowledge argument.[50] The reasons for this derive from the so-called "Flicker Defense" against Frankfurt-like scenarios developed by more typical incompatibilists.[51] What advocates of this defense emphasize is that so long as it is granted that Frankfurt-like scenarios are ones in which causal determinism does not hold, it must also be granted that there will be *some* alternatives available to S in these scenarios.[52] The alternatives may be so simple as those in which S does A of S's own volition and those in which S does A as a result of the intervening mechanism. If we assume that the scenarios do not involve causal determinism, then there will be such alternatives. And, of course, the only Frankfurt-like scenarios in which an *incompatibilist* is willing to grant the subject has freedom will be scenarios in which causal determinism does not hold. Thus, in every Frankfurt-like scenario in which an incompatibilist will grant that the subject has freedom, the incompatibilist must grant that *some* alternatives are available to the subject.

The alternatives available might not be the alternatives stated in the Principle of Accidental Possibilities presented earlier. For, it might be that in every alternative possibility available, S in fact *does* A. Thus, S's doing A is accidentally necessary. However, exactly what the alternatives are is of little concern for present purposes,

---

[46] See, e.g., Fischer (2002 and 2010).

[47] E.g., Stump (1999 and 2001), Zagzebski (2000), Hunt (2000), and Pereboom (2001).

[48] For discussion of how these so-called "Frankfurt-libertarians" run against the grain of typical incompatibilism, see Hasker (1999) and Wierenga (2007).

[49] For an attempt to supply what is needed, see Pereboom (2001).

[50] For a parallel discussion which also emphasizes different *versions* of PAP, see Timpe (2006a).

[51] See, e.g., Kane (1998), Widerker (1995), Ginet (1996) and Goetz (2005).

[52] This is what is emphasized, anyway, by advocates of what Timpe (2006b) calls the "weak" flicker strategy.

because God will not only know *that* S will do A, but God will know everything there is to know about S's doing A. Thus, for example, God will know whether S will do A of S's own volition or whether S will do A as a result of an intervening mechanism. So, if the foreknowledge argument succeeds up to claim (7), it will follow that not only is S's doing A accidentally necessary, but every detail about *how* S does A is accidentally necessary as well. Yet, if every detail about how S does A is accidentally necessary, then there are *no* alternative accidental possibilities of *any* kind for S's action. And, as we've seen, no incompatibilist can maintain that *this* is consistent with S's performing S's action freely. The concern, then, is that even if Frankfurt-like scenarios could offer the incompatibilist reason to reject (7), they cannot offer her reason to reject a parallel claim which can be used to construct an only slightly modified version of the foreknowledge argument. So the present strategy is not a success.

4. Conclusion

In this chapter we began with a careful presentation of the foreknowledge argument, an argument which attempts to show that God's having exhaustive and infallible foreknowledge of the future actions of creatures implies that those actions are not done freely. We compared this argument to two similar arguments, the arguments for logical and causal fatalism. We then explored a variety of responses to the foreknowledge argument which either deny one of its premises or dispute one if its inferences.

There are two lessons I hope the reader will take away from the chapter. The first is concerned with the standards for success we established for responses to the foreknowledge argument. We established, first, that a successful response to the foreknowledge argument must not merely show that a premise in the argument is false or that an inference in the argument is fallacious. Rather, the response must also not be vulnerable to only slightly modified versions of the foreknowledge argument which also threaten to demonstrate the impossibility of upholding the motivations to affirm divine cognitive perfection and significant creaturely freedom. Second, we established that a successful response to the foreknowledge argument must explain why it is typically thought that the foreknowledge argument is more powerful than the argument for logical fatalism. And, third, we established that, other things being equal, it would be preferable if a response to the foreknowledge argument did not threaten the argument for causal fatalism, or at least the basic idea behind that argument, just as much as it threatened the foreknowledge argument.

The second lesson is that, despite the various ingenious responses to the foreknowledge argument we surveyed which deny a premise or dispute an inference in the argument, it is far from clear that any of them meets our standards for success. While several of these responses contain promising insights, and perhaps plausibly accomplish some of what is required for a successful response to the foreknowledge argument, it is quite disputable that any of them accomplishes all that is required by our standards. This lesson may initially sound like a cause for alarm for those desiring a successful response to the foreknowledge argument. For, if none of the ways here surveyed for denying a premise or disputing an inference in the argument is successful, and if these ways surveyed are representative of the total available ways, then how could *any* response to the argument be successful? My hope in the remainder of this book is to address this very question by showing that there is available a successful response to the foreknowledge argument which doesn't involve denying a premise of the argument or disputing one of its inferences.

2

Foreknowledge and Explaining
the Absence of Freedom[1]

In the previous chapter, we articulated a careful version of the foreknowledge argument, identified success conditions governing responses to that argument, and examined responses to it that reject one of its premises or inferences. The three success conditions we identified were as follows. First, a successful response must not merely identify a technical flaw in the foreknowledge argument thereby leaving open the success of an only slightly modified version of that argument. Second, a successful response must accommodate the widely shared idea that the foreknowledge argument has more going for it than the argument for logical fatalism. And, third, a successful response must not threaten the argument for causal fatalism, or the basic idea behind it, as much as it threatens the foreknowledge argument. We saw in Chapter 1 that, arguably, none of the responses to the foreknowledge argument which deny one of its premises or inferences satisfies all three of these criteria.

Someone zealous to find a successful response to the foreknowledge argument might take this result to be a brutal blow against his project. If the responses to the foreknowledge argument surveyed in Chapter 1 are exhaustive or even representative of possible responses, then the prospects for finding a successful response to the foreknowledge argument seem bleak indeed. Nonetheless it turns out that several authors have not treated the results of Chapter 1 in this way. Well aware of the difficulties facing responses to the foreknowledge argument which deny one of its premises or inferences, they remain unimpressed by the argument. David Hunt (1999), for example, finds it "preposterous" to think that divine foreknowledge by itself could undermine freedom.[2] He goes on to claim that "the supposed incompatibility of divine foreknowledge and human freedom lacks all prima facie credibility" (20). Hunt suggests that we treat the foreknowledge argument in much the same way as one might treat one of Zeno's famed arguments, such as his argument for the conclusion that nothing can move. Even if we are not confident about any particular response to this argument which denies one of its premises or inferences, we may be perfectly rational not to believe the argument to be sound if we find its conclusion utterly incredible. Similarly, an author may perfectly rationally find it incredible that he has made no

---

[1] I first presented the central argument of this chapter in Byerly (2012b). The presentation here has been revised and updated, however.
[2] Compare Craig (1987) and Hunt (1998).

mistakes in his work even though he is not confident of any particular affirmation within that work that it is mistaken.[3] Those who are sympathetic with this sort of response to the foreknowledge argument think that *its* conclusion is incredible enough to justify rejecting the argument's soundness, even if they cannot identify precisely where it fails. They wonder: How *could* the fact that anyone, even God, knows what a person will do show that this person could not have done what she does freely?

In this book I want to develop a strategy for responding to the foreknowledge argument, which is sympathetic with the concern voiced by the foregoing authors. The foregoing authors want to know what it is about infallible and exhaustive divine foreknowledge (below, I will often simply write, "divine foreknowledge") that *makes* human beings lack freedom. And the strategy I will develop focuses on this very concern about the explanation for why human beings lack freedom. It proposes, first, that we are in a position to know that the foreknowledge argument is sound only if we are in a position to know that divine foreknowledge requires the existence of something which *makes* it the case that no person performs any action freely. It then proposes that we are not in a position to know that divine foreknowledge requires the existence of something which makes persons lack freedom. This is because the best candidate proposals for what is both required by divine foreknowledge and removes freedom are all either such that we do not know that they are required by divine foreknowledge or we do not know that their existence makes persons lack freedom.

This chapter explores three initially attractive proposals for that which is both required by divine foreknowledge and which explains the absence of human freedom. In Section 1, I begin by briefly explaining why we should think that the foreknowledge argument's soundness hinges on whether divine foreknowledge requires something that makes humans lack freedom in the first place. I show more specifically why the success of this argument depends upon whether divine foreknowledge requires the existence of something which explains why human beings lack alternative possibilities. I then go on to show in that section that what is required by divine foreknowledge and explains why human beings lack alternative possibilities cannot be either the mental component or the truth component of divine foreknowledge. Section 2 then introduces the proposal that what is required by divine foreknowledge and makes human beings lack alternative possibilities is instead the truth of causal determinism. I argue that this proposal is not only better than the two proposals of Section 1, but that it is the *best* proposal we know of for that which is both required by divine foreknowledge and which explains the absence of alternative possibilities. Part of the explanation for why the truth of causal determinism is the best known proposal here is that there is a powerful inductive argument for the conclusion that divine foreknowledge indeed requires the truth of causal determinism. It turns out that the success of the strategy I aim to develop depends upon the advocate of that strategy developing a response to the aforementioned inductive argument. Much of the remainder of this book is accordingly devoted to developing just such a response. I aim to show that, in spite of the power of this inductive argument, we are not in a position to know that divine

---

[3]   See Makinson (1965).

foreknowledge requires the truth of causal determinism. Since the truth of causal determinism is the best proposal we know of for that which is both required by divine foreknowledge and explains the absence of alternative possibilities, we are not in a position to know that there is something that is both required by divine foreknowledge and explains the absence of alternative possibilities. Thus, we are not in a position to know that the foreknowledge argument is sound.

1. Explaining the absence of freedom through the mental and truth components of divine foreknowledge

Two observations will make it clear why it is dialectically innocent to affirm that the soundness of the foreknowledge argument depends upon whether divine foreknowledge requires something which explains the absence of alternative possibilities. The first observation is that every version of the foreknowledge argument attempts to establish that the existence of divine foreknowledge shows that there are no free actions because it shows that there are no relevant alternative possibilities for any action performed by any human being. Certain assumptions may vary from one version of the foreknowledge argument to the next. One may make use of divine beliefs while another uses divine awarenesses; one may require divine temporality while another permits divine atemporality; one may use accidental necessity and another, uncausability; and one may appeal to one sort of alternatives while another appeals to a different sort of alternatives. But what every version has in common is that it attempts to establish that the existence of divine foreknowledge shows that human actions are not free because a certain relevant kind of alternative to those actions is not available.

The second observation is that members of my target audience will not affirm that it is intrinsically impossible that there be alternative possibilities for human actions. Those I have in mind here are, on the one hand, advocates of the foreknowledge argument who think this argument makes a difference and, on the other hand, those traditional theists attracted to incompatibilism who wish to find a response to the foreknowledge argument. Advocates of the foreknowledge argument who think it makes a difference will have to maintain that free action requires alternative possibilities. And, since they will not claim that free action is intrinsically impossible, neither will they claim that the relevant sort of alternative possibilities are intrinsically impossible. Similarly, theists attracted to incompatibilism will all affirm that free action requires some sort of alternative possibilities. And, in order to maintain the free will defense against the logical problem of evil, they will have to maintain that free action, is at least *possible*. Thus, they will have to maintain that alternative possibilities are intrinsically possible.

The two foregoing observations render it dialectically innocent to affirm that if the foreknowledge argument is sound, then divine foreknowledge requires the existence of something which explains the absence of alternative possibilities. The reason for this is that, given that the target audience here affirms that relevant alternative possibilities are possible, they will very likely think that if there are no relevant alternative possibilities, there is an explanation for this fact. There is, minimally, a strong prima facie presumption that if a fact is contingent, then there is an explanation for it—something makes it so.[4] However, all versions of the foreknowledge argument maintain that the existence of divine foreknowledge shows that there are no alternative possibilities. Thus, if the foreknowledge argument is sound, there must be an explanation for why there are no alternative possibilities. In other words, if the foreknowledge argument is sound, then the existence of divine foreknowledge requires something which explains why alternative possibilities required for free action are unavailable.

Establishing the dialectical innocence of the claim that the soundness of the foreknowledge argument depends upon whether divine foreknowledge requires something which explains the absence of alternative possibilities is the first step in pursuing the strategy outlined in the introduction to this chapter. The second step for pursuing this strategy is to argue that the best candidates for that which is both required by divine foreknowledge and explains the absence of alternative possibilities either are all such that we do not know that they are required by divine foreknowledge or they are such that we do not know that they explain the absence of alternative possibilities. I begin to pursue this step in this section by considering two proposals for that which is both required by divine foreknowledge and explains the absence of alternative possibilities. The two proposals are, respectively, the mental component of divine foreknowledge and the truth component of divine foreknowledge. I argue that these proposals fail because we do not know that they explain the absence of alternative possibilities. The next section develops a better proposal with which I will engage for the remainder of this text.

First, suppose someone suggested that whatever divine mental state is involved in achieving divine foreknowledge is that which is required by divine foreknowledge and which also explains why human beings lack alternative possibilities. This mental state might be a divine belief, a divine awareness, a divine intuition, or some other sort of divine mental state whereby foreknowledge is achieved. The advocate of this first approach claims that such a mental state is required for God to achieve foreknowledge and that God's hosting this mental state explains why there are no alternative possibilities for human actions. It is God's hosting such mental state that makes human beings lack freedom. Thus, to return to our example from the previous chapter, it is God's believing that Elizabeth sings her sonnet to John at t_{100} that explains why Elizabeth's singing is not done freely.

There is very good reason to doubt the explanatory claim in this proposal. We can see why by attending to the options available concerning the explanatory relationship between God's hosting the relevant mental state on the one hand and the actions of human beings on the other. Thus, in the example from Chapter 1, we can see why this proposal fails by attending to the options concerning the explanatory relationship between God's belief that Elizabeth sings a sonnet to John at t_{100} and Elizabeth's singing this sonnet. There are four options for how God's belief and Elizabeth's singing might

---

[4] For a detailed defense of principles of sufficient reason such as this one, see Pruss (2006).

be related explanatorily. But, the two which are most independently attractive will not permit God's forebelief to explain why Elizabeth lacks freedom.

Let us begin with the two more independently attractive options for answering our question about the explanatory relationship between God's belief and Elizabeth's singing. The first alternative is to affirm that Elizabeth's singing at t_{100} explains God's forebelieving at t_1 that Elizabeth sings at t_{100}. This answer to our explanation question has been almost universally affirmed by those who think that creaturely freedom and infallible divine foreknowledge are consistent.[5] It is an independently attractive option for answering our explanation question. But, this alternative will not permit the mental component of divine foreknowledge to explain the absence of human freedom. For, strikingly, if this answer to our explanation question is given, then the supposition that God's forebelief about Elizabeth explains why Elizabeth lacks freedom leads to an absurdity, given the plausible assumption that explanations are transitive.

To say that explanations are transitive is to say the following: for all explanations e, e′, and e″, if e explains e′ and e′ explains e″, then e explains e″. The claim that explanations are transitive, like the claim that causes are transitive, has enjoyed widespread support, and it seems to make good sense of many ordinary examples.[6] For instance, if I was late for the morning session because I felt sick, and I felt sick because I ate some bad fish last night, then I was late for the morning session because I ate some bad fish last night. If my moving my arm in a certain way explains why the marker moves in an "R" pattern in contact with the board, and the marker's moving in this pattern explains why there is an "R" pattern of ink on the board, then my moving my arm in a certain way explains why there is an "R" pattern of ink on the board. Transitivity appears to hold even when some of the explanations involved are (at least apparently) backwards explanations.[7] If the volcano is smoking because it is going to explode, and the people are leaving because the volcano is smoking, then the people are leaving because the volcano is going to explode.

Suppose, then, that explanations are indeed transitive. We now run into an absurdity, given this first option concerning the explanatory relationship between God's forebelief and Elizabeth's singing, if we wish to maintain that divine forebelief explains the absence of human freedom. For, on this first option, Elizabeth's singing at t_{100} is said to explain God's forebelief at t_1 that Elizabeth sings at t_{100}. But, if divine forebelief is to explain the absence of human freedom, then it must be that God's forebelief at t_1 that Elizabeth sings at t_{100} explains why Elizabeth can't do otherwise

---

[5]   To see this, consider what a wide variety of solutions to the freedom-foreknowledge argument have endorsed this idea that divine (fore)beliefs are explained by what makes their contents true: Augustinian solutions (see Hunt (1999), Boethian solutions (see Rota 2010), Molinist solutions (Merricks 2011b), and Ockhamist solutions (see Plantinga 1986)). Merricks (2009) goes so far as to suggest that it is this insight alone which is enough to make for a successful response to the foreknowledge argument.

[6]   For the transitivity of causation, see Hall (2000). For the transitivity of explanation, see Hasker (1997).

[7]   For a defense of the ubiquity of legitimate backward explanations, see Jenkins and Nolan (2008). For a criticism of this defense, see Byerly (2013).

than sing at t_{100}. Thus, given the transitivity of explanations, it follows that Elizabeth's singing at t_{100} explains why Elizabeth can't do otherwise than sing at t_{100}. Elizabeth's singing at t_{100} makes it the case that she doesn't sing freely at t_{100}. But, this is absurd! So, we must reject one of the suppositions which got us to this conclusion. Given that explanations are transitive, we must either reject the claim that God's forebelief explains why Elizabeth lacks freedom, or we must reject the claim that Elizabeth's singing at t_{100} explains God's forebelief that Elizabeth sings. This first option for answering our question about the explanatory relationship between divine belief and human action, then, while independently attractive, cannot be offered by someone who wants to defend the idea that divine forebelief explains the absence of human freedom.

There is a second option for answering our question which is still somewhat independently attractive. On this option, Elizabeth's singing and God's forebelieving that Elizabeth sings share a common explanation. What explains God's forebeliefs about Elizabeth's singing and what explains Elizabeth's singing is one and the same, though neither Elizabeth's singing nor God's forebelief explains the other. Apart from the first answer to our question posed earlier according to which Elizabeth's singing explains God's forebelief about her singing, this may be the most popular response to our question about the explanatory relationship between divine forebelief and human action.

There are at least two ways of pursuing this answer to our question of which I am aware in the philosophical literature—a Molinist account of divine foreknowledge and a Theological Determinist account of divine foreknowledge.[8] The details of these accounts needn't concern us much here. For, quite apart from these details, it is clear that this strategy of answering our question about the explanatory relationship between divine forebelief and human action will not permit divine forebelief itself to be that which explains why human actions are not done freely. According to such accounts, if anything explains why human beings lack alternatives to their actions, it will be that which is the common explanation for both divine forebelief and human action. For example, on the Molinist account, this might be the brute fact[9] of certain subjunctive conditionals concerning what persons would do in certain circumstances together with God's having actualized those circumstances; and, on the determinist account it might be God's having causally determined the actions to occur. But on neither account will it be divine forebelief which explains why human actions are not done freely. Divine forebelief is a vestigial by-product of that which explains human action and the presence or absence of freedom in human action in such views.

So much for the two answers to our question about the explanatory relationship between divine forebelief and human action which are somewhat independently

---

[8]   For standard defenses of Molinism, see Flint (1998) and Craig (1990). Standard defenses of Theological Determinism are lacking in the philosophical literature; though, see Wainwright (2001) and Rudder-Baker (2003) and McCann (1995).

[9]   For a discussion of the view that subjunctive conditionals are brute facts, see Adams (1977).

attractive. The other two answers to this question, while they might allow for more hope concerning divine forebelief explaining the absence of human freedom, nonetheless suffer because they are independently implausible as answers to the question.

Suppose, first, that one answers our question by claiming that God's forebelief explains why Elizabeth sings. Elizabeth sings at t_{100} because God believes at t_1 that Elizabeth sings at t_{100}. This response to our question has perhaps the best shot at permitting divine forebelief to explain why human actions are not up to us. Unfortunately, this answer to our question about the explanatory relationship between God's forebelief and Elizabeth's singing has not been popular at all.[10] And, its unpopularity is for good reason. I will briefly discuss two problems for this account here which help to show why it is not an independently plausible response to our explanation question.

First, this account succumbs to a suspicious form of anti-realism. On this response to our question, God's beliefs determine how reality is. For, presumably, it will not be just Elizabeth's singing that occurs because God believes it will occur, but *any* event is like this. For every event that occurs or doesn't occur in the history of the world, it occurs because God believed it would occur or it doesn't occur because God believed it wouldn't occur. This view is objectionable, however. For, it seems that, even if *per impossibile*, were God to have decided *not* to hold a belief about whether Elizabeth will sing at t_{100}, Elizabeth still would have either sung or not sung at t_{100}.[11] Insofar as one finds this sort of anti-realism unattractive, as this author does, she will not want to advocate this answer to our question about the explanatory relationship between God's forebelief and Elizabeth's singing.

A second difficulty with this response to our question has to do with its commitment to massive explanatory overdetermination. Elizabeth sings at t_{100}, according to this response, because God believed *at t_1* that she would sing at t_{100}. But, why is t_1 so important? Why not pick some other time at which God believed that Elizabeth would sing at t_{100}? Why not, for that matter, pick t_{100} itself? Presumably, at t_{100}, God believes that Elizabeth sings at t_{100}. Why think that it is God's beliefs at t_1 that explain why Elizabeth sings and not God's beliefs at t_{100} instead? Of course, it could be that God's beliefs at *both* these times—indeed, at *all* of the times—explain why Elizabeth sings. But, here again this answer to our question seems to have, if anything, gotten things backwards.

---

[10] Some will suggest that Aquinas countenances such a view in *Summa Theologica* I, Q.14.A8. However, even this attribution is suspect, as Merricks (2009) makes clear.

[11] I say "even if *per impossibile*" because some, including myself, think that it is metaphysically impossible for God to fail to have a belief about whether Joe will mow. They think that it is necessary that either Joe will mow or Joe will not mow and that it is necessary that if Joe will mow God believed this and if Joe will not mow God believed that. If this is correct, then the conditional claim <were God to have decided not to hold a belief about whether Joe will mow, Joe still would have either mowed or not mowed> has an impossible antecedent. But, many, including myself, think that not all counterpossible claims like this are trivially true, though on some semantics for counterpossibles this is the case (see, e.g., (Lewis 1973)). Instead, we think that some counterpossibles are non-trivially true and some are false. The counterpossible claim in the text, I contend, is non-trivially true. Yet, given the response to our explanation question we are considering in the text, this conditional cannot be true. I take this as an objection to that answer to our explanation question. For more in defense of the non-trivial truth and falsity of counterpossible conditionals, see Merricks (2003), Berto (2009), and Vander Laan (2004).

Given this answer to our question, when we ask why Elizabeth sang at t_{100}, our answer will be that she sang at t_{100} because of what God believed at t_1 and because of what God believed at t_2 and because of what God believed at t_3 and so on for every other time (perhaps including even the future times). But, this highlights a second unattractive feature of the present response to our question. For this response unnecessarily adopts massive explanatory overdetermination. Elizabeth's singing at t_{100}, and any event at any time for that matter, will be massively explanatorily overdetermined by God's beliefs at every time. A response to our explanation question, like the first two responses we considered, which didn't require such massive explanatory overdetermination, is far more independently attractive than this third answer.[12] Thus, despite its potential promise for defending the idea that divine forebelief explains the absence of human freedom, the present response to our question about the explanatory relationship between divine forebelief and human action should be rejected as independently unattractive in light of its commitments to anti-realism and unnecessary explanatory overdetermination.

There is one final available response to our question: claim that there is simply *no* explanatory relationship at all between God's infallible forebelief that Elizabeth will sing and Elizabeth's singing. God doesn't believe that Elizabeth will sing because Elizabeth will sing, nor will Elizabeth sing because God believes Elizabeth will sing, nor is there a common explanation for both God's belief and Elizabeth's singing. This answer to our question, I submit, is woefully independently unattractive. It is woefully independently unattractive because it implies that something which should be explicable is inexplicable. For, what this response says about the relationship between God's forebelief about Elizabeth and Elizabeth's singing its advocates will also need to say about the relationship between any of God's forebeliefs about what humans will do and what these humans will do. Thus, for any proposition p concerning what a human being will do, the advocate of this solution will say that God will believe p if and only if p is true, but there will be no explanation of why this is so. The correspondence between divine beliefs about what humans will do and what humans will do is left entirely unexplained. It simply happens to be that for every claim p about what a human will do, God believes p if and only if p is true. God doesn't believe p because it is true, nor is p true because God believes it, nor is there some common explanation for why both p is true and God believes p. It just happens to be that divine beliefs and human acts correspond. This commitment to the inexplicability of what cries out for explanation makes this final alternative woefully independently unattractive. There must be some kind of explanatory relation between divine forebeliefs concerning human actions and what humans do. The only explanatory relationships there might be, however, have already been surveyed. And for each of these relationships, either the relationship proposed is independently unattractive or it will not permit divine

---

[12] That a view countenances massive and unnecessary explanatory overdetermination is commonly thought to be a significant reason for rejecting that view. For some representative samples of arguments which invoke explanatory overdetermination in this way, see Merricks (2003), Kim (2005), and Korman (2011).

forebelief to explain the absence of human freedom. Thus, I conclude that there is no independently attractive response to our question about the relationship between divine forebelief and human action which will permit divine forebelief to explain the absence of human freedom. Plausibly, then, divine forebelief cannot explain the absence of human freedom. If the foreknowledge argument is sound, it must be that infallible divine foreknowledge requires something *else* which explains the absence of human freedom.

A second proposal concerning that which is both required by divine foreknowledge and which explains why human actions are not performed freely is the truth component of divine foreknowledge. Since knowledge requires the truth of what is known, divine foreknowledge concerning human actions will require the truth of the claims which are believed, or of which God is aware, etc., regarding human actions. In our example from Chapter 1, the proposal here is that it is the *truth* of the claim <Elizabeth sings a love sonnet to John at t_{100}> which is required in order for God to know that Elizabeth sings to John at t_{100} and which makes it the case that Elizabeth does not sing her love sonnet to John *freely* at t_{100}. The latter conjunct here will hold, it is proposed, because the truth of <Elizabeth sings a love sonnet to John at t_{100}> at t_1 explains why Elizabeth lacks alternative possibilities at t_{100}.

I want to urge two difficulties for this proposal. The first is that this response appears to place the foreknowledge argument and the argument for logical fatalism on equal footing. If the reason why divine foreknowledge threatens human freedom is just that it requires that there be true claims about what humans do long before they do it, then the foreknowledge argument is exactly as strong as the argument for logical fatalism. But, we saw in Chapter 1 that this is an undesirable result, since most who have worked on the foreknowledge argument have thought that it is more appealing than the argument for logical fatalism. At the very least, the present approach to explaining what it is which is both required by divine foreknowledge and which makes human beings lack freedom needs to be supplemented with an explanation about why many experts are wrongly tempted to think that the foreknowledge argument is more appealing than the argument for logical fatalism.

The second difficulty for this approach is that it is subject to an argument which parallels the argument developed earlier in response to the first proposal about divine forebelief. When we attended to the question about the explanatory relationship between divine forebelief and human action, we saw that of four available answers to this question, the only independently attractive answers were ones which would not permit divine forebelief to explain why human actions are not performed freely. A similar result obtains when we ask about the explanatory relationship between the past truth of propositions about what humans will do and what humans do. This result obtains, for example, when we ask about the explanatory relationship between the truth at t_1 of <Elizabeth sings a love sonnet to John at t_{100}> and Elizabeth's singing a love sonnet to John at t_{100}. There are four possible answers to this question. But, the only two independently attractive answers are ones which will not permit the truth of the proposition in question to be that which explains why Elizabeth's singing is not done freely.

Let us begin with the two more attractive answers to our question. The first answer affirms that Elizabeth's singing at t_{100} explains the truth at t_1 of <Elizabeth sings a love sonnet to John at t_{100}>. This answer to our explanation question has been very commonly affirmed by those working on truth and freedom.[13] It is a tempting answer especially for those who are attracted to the view that truth supervenes on being—that what is true depends upon the way the world is. Here, the truth of <Elizabeth sings a love sonnet to John at t_{100}> at t_1 or at any other time depends upon the way the world is at t_{100}—specifically, it depends upon whether Elizabeth sings a love sonnet to John at t_{100}. Despite its attraction, this answer to our question will not permit the truth component of divine foreknowledge to explain the absence of human freedom. For, strikingly, if this answer to our explanatory question is given, then the supposition that the truth at t_1 of <Elizabeth sings a love sonnet to John at t_{100}> explains why Elizabeth lacks freedom leads to an absurdity, given the plausible assumption that explanations are transitive. The absurdity that follows, given these commitments, is that Elizabeth's singing a love sonnet to John at t_{100} explains why Elizabeth cannot do otherwise at t_{100}. Her singing itself will explain why she doesn't sing freely. This absurdity follows from the conjunction of (i) the supposition that explanations are transitive, (ii) the commitment of the present proposal that the truth at t_1 of <Elizabeth sings a love sonnet to John at t_{100}> explains why Elizabeth lacks alternative possibilities, and (iii) the present approach to answering our explanatory question which affirms that Elizabeth's singing at t_{100} explains the truth at t_1 of <Elizabeth sings a love sonnet to John at t_{100}>.

There is a second option for answering our question which some, though fewer than those who are attracted to the first answer, have still found somewhat independently attractive.[14] On this option, Elizabeth's singing and the truth at t_1 of <Elizabeth sings a love sonnet to John at t_{100}> share a common explanation. What explains the truth at t_1 of <Elizabeth sings a love sonnet to John at t_{100}> and what explains Elizabeth's singing at t_{100} is one and the same, though neither Elizabeth's singing nor the truth at t_1 of <Elizabeth sings a love sonnet to John at t_{100}> explains the other. The common explanation for both Elizabeth's singing at t_{100} and the truth at t_1 of <Elizabeth sings a love sonnet to John at t_{100}> is the existence at t_1 of conditions which causally determine Elizabeth to sing to John at t_{100}. In accordance with the Piercean semantics for propositions about the future discussed in Chapter 1, it is only because such causally determining conditions are present at t_1 that it is true at t_1 that <Elizabeth sings a love sonnet to John at t_{100}>. And, further, Elizabeth in fact does sing to John at t_{100} because these conditions were present at t_1.

It should be clear that this strategy of answering our question about the explanatory relationship between the truth component of divine foreknowledge and human action will not permit the truth component of divine foreknowledge itself to be that which explains why human actions are not done freely. According to the present proposal, if anything explains why human beings lack alternatives to their actions, it will be that

---

[13] Merricks (2009) is an excellent example.

[14] See Rhoda (2007) and the references he cites in favor of the Piercean semantics for excellent examples.

which is the common explanation for both the truth component of divine foreknowledge and the occurrence of human actions. It will be, in other words, the existence at t_1 of conditions which causally determine Elizabeth to sing at t_{100} which explains why her singing is not done freely. The truth component of divine foreknowledge is merely a vestigial byproduct of that which explains human action and the presence or absence of freedom in human action, according to this proposal.

So much for the two answers to our question about the explanatory relationship between the truth component of divine foreknowledge and human action which are somewhat independently attractive. The other two answers to this question, while they might allow for more hope concerning the truth component of divine foreknowledge explaining the absence of human freedom, nonetheless suffer because they are independently implausible as answers to the question.

Suppose, first, that one answers our question by claiming that the truth at t_1 of <Elizabeth sings a love sonnet to John at t_{100}> explains why Elizabeth sings at t_{100}. Elizabeth sings at t_{100} because <Elizabeth sings a love sonnet to John at t_{100}> is true at t_1. This response to our question has perhaps the best shot at permitting the truth component of divine foreknowledge to explain why human actions are not up to us. Unfortunately, this answer to our question about the explanatory relationship between God's forebelief and Elizabeth's singing has not been popular at all.[15] And, its unpopularity is for good reason.

The primary difficulty with this proposal is that it simply gets the explanatory relationship between truth and reality backwards. It is reality—what there is—that explains what is true, not the other way around. This difficulty is perhaps most striking if we consider what the present proposal would appear to have to say about the truth of <Elizabeth sings a love sonnet to John at t_{100}> *at t_{100}*. Presumably, just as the advocate of this strategy proposes that the truth of <Elizabeth sings a love sonnet to John at t_{100}> *at t_1* and other times earlier than t_{100} explains Elizabeth's singing at t_{100}, she will also say that the truth of <Elizabeth sings a love sonnet to John at t_{100}> *at t_{100}* explains why Elizabeth sings at t_{100}.[16] But, then, if she wants to claim that the truth of <Elizabeth sings a love sonnet to John at t_{100}> at times earlier than t_{100} makes Elizabeth lack freedom at t_{100}, it would appear she must likewise say that the truth of <Elizabeth sings a love sonnet to John at t_{100}> *at t_{100}* makes Elizabeth lack freedom at t_{100}. Surely this result is undesirable. So, while the present approach to addressing the explanatory relationship between the truth component of divine foreknowledge and human action may permit some hope for defending the claim that the truth component of divine foreknowledge explains why humans lack freedom, this approach is nonetheless independently unattractive.

There is one final available response to our question: claim that there is simply *no* explanatory relationship at all between the truth component of divine foreknowledge and Elizabeth's singing at t_{100}. It isn't true at t_1 that <Elizabeth sings a love sonnet to John

---

[15] See discussion in Merricks (2009).

[16] Other options face serious difficulties. For example, if she claimed that Elizabeth's singing at t_{100} explains why it is true at t_{100} that <Elizabeth sings a love sonnet to John at t_{100}>, then given the transitivity of explanations she would have to countenance circular explanations.

at t_{100}> because Elizabeth sings at t_{100}, nor does Elizabeth sing at t_{100} because <Elizabeth sings a love sonnet to John at t_{100}> is true at t_1, nor is there a common explanation for both the truth at t_1 of <Elizabeth sings a love sonnet to John at t_{100}> and Elizabeth's singing at t_{100}. This answer to our question, I submit, is woefully independently unattractive. It is woefully independently unattractive because it implies that something which should be explicable is inexplicable. For, what this response says about the relationship between the foretruth of <Elizabeth sings a love sonnet to John at t_{100}> and Elizabeth's singing at t_{100} its advocates will also need to say about the relationship between the foretruth of any proposition about the future actions of human beings and what these persons will do. Thus, for any proposition p asserting that a human being S does some action A at a future time t, the advocate of this solution will say that p will have been true in the past if and only if S does A at t, but there will be no explanation of why this is so. The correspondence between the foretruth of propositions about what humans will do and what humans will do is left entirely unexplained. It just happens to be that the foretruth of propositions about what humans will do and future human acts correspond. This commitment to the inexplicability of what cries out for explanation makes this final alternative woefully independently unattractive. There must be some kind of explanatory relation between the foretruth of propositions concerning future human actions and what humans will do. The only explanatory relationships there might be, however, have already been surveyed. And for each of these relationships, either the relationship proposed is independently unattractive or it will not permit the truth component of divine foreknowledge to explain the absence of human freedom. Thus, I conclude that there is no independently attractive response to our question about the relationship between the truth component of divine foreknowledge and human action which will permit the truth component of divine foreknowledge to explain the absence of human freedom. Plausibly, then, the truth component of divine foreknowledge cannot explain the absence of human freedom. Thus, given our previous result, neither the mental component nor the truth component of divine foreknowledge can explain why human beings lack freedom. So, if the foreknowledge argument is sound, there must be something other than the mental component and the truth component of divine foreknowledge which is both required by this foreknowledge and which explains why human beings lack freedom.

2. Causal determinism and the foreknowledge argument

If neither the mental component nor the truth component of divine foreknowledge is what explains why human beings lack freedom, then what could it be that is both required by divine foreknowledge and that explains why human beings lack freedom? In this section, I want to propose that the best answer to this question we know of is the truth of causal determinism. This is for two reasons.

The first reason why the truth of causal determinism is a promising proposal for that which is both required by divine foreknowledge and which explains the absence of human freedom is that those who are most hard-pressed to find a response to the foreknowledge argument are likely to agree that the truth of causal determinism indeed *would* explain the absence of human freedom. This is because those who are most troubled by the foreknowledge argument are traditional theists attracted to incompatibilism about freedom and causal determinism. They hold that if causal determinism were true, there couldn't be any free actions; and, they tend to think that the truth of causal determinism would explain why human actions could not be done freely. Thus, if the defender of the foreknowledge argument were to propose that it is the truth of causal determinism which is both required by divine foreknowledge and explains why human beings lack freedom, then at least with respect to the second conjunct here—the claim that the truth of causal determinism explains the absence of human freedom—she would gain a dialectical advantage. *If* she can show that the first conjunct holds, too—that divine foreknowledge indeed does require the truth of causal determinism—then those who are most hard-pressed to find a response to her argument will be left without one. They will have to grant that infallible divine foreknowledge is after all incompatible with human freedom, since it requires something they are antecedently committed to claiming would rule out human freedom. Thus, the proposal that the truth of causal determinism is that which is required by divine foreknowledge and explains the absence of human freedom is dialectically attractive.

The second reason why the truth of causal determinism is a promising proposal for that which is both required by divine foreknowledge and which explains the absence of human freedom is that there is a powerful argument for the conclusion that divine foreknowledge indeed *does* require the truth of causal determinism. Thus, not only is it dialectically attractive for the advocate of the foreknowledge argument to claim that the truth of causal determinism would explain why human beings lack freedom, but there is available to her a powerful argument for the claim that divine foreknowledge requires the truth of causal determinism. By proposing that it is the truth of causal determinism which is both required by divine foreknowledge and which explains the absence of human freedom, the advocate of the foreknowledge argument will surely put those aiming to respond to this argument on the defensive. Their only option will be to respond to her argument that divine foreknowledge requires the truth of causal determinism.

I will present the argument that divine foreknowledge requires the truth of causal determinism momentarily. But before doing so, I want to emphasize why the present proposal is not only promising, but the *best* proposal available for an advocate of the foreknowledge argument. The goal of an advocate of the foreknowledge argument in making a proposal about that which is both required by divine foreknowledge and which explains the absence of human freedom is to propose something which she will be well-positioned to argue is both (i) required by divine foreknowledge and (ii) would explain the absence of human freedom if it obtained. The proposal of the truth of causal determinism puts the advocate of the foreknowledge argument in the best possible position with respect to (ii), since *by definition* her key opponents will grant that the truth of causal determinism would explain the absence of human freedom. Further, the proposal of the truth of causal determinism, as we will see momentarily, positions the advocate of the foreknowledge argument well with respect to (i), since there is available to her a powerful argument for the claim that infallible divine foreknowledge requires the truth of causal determinism. No other proposal we know of positions the advocate of the foreknowledge argument equally well with respect to (i) and (ii). For, any other proposal will be one which requires an argumentative defense that the proposal achieves (i) *as well as* an argumentative defense that the proposal achieves (ii). It will not simply follow by definition that the proposal accomplishes either (i) *or* (ii). Thus, any other proposal we know of will be one where the opponent of the foreknowledge argument will have more room to object, making the present proposal the best proposal we know of.

The foregoing defense of the claim that the truth of causal determinism is the best proposal we know of for that which is both required by divine foreknowledge and which explains the absence of human freedom depends crucially on the claim that there indeed is a powerful argument that divine foreknowledge requires the truth of causal determinism. So, I must now turn to that argument. The best argument I know of for the claim that divine foreknowledge requires the truth of causal determinism is an inductive argument based on our knowledge of how foreknowledge of contingent claims about the future is obtained.

The only way of obtaining foreknowledge of contingent claims about the future that we know of is to obtain such foreknowledge on the basis of one's knowledge of the past and the laws of nature. For instance, I might know that it will rain in Mississippi tomorrow morning on the basis of my knowledge that it rained earlier this evening in Texas and my knowledge of the law-like behavior of weather patterns in the southeastern United States. I might know that the formerly blue litmus paper will be red in a few minutes on the basis of my knowledge that the paper was just sprinkled with acid and my knowledge of the laws governing the interaction of acid and litmus paper. In each case, I might not know a whole lot about the relevant laws; but it is only insofar as I have some grasp of them, even if I don't think of them *as laws*, that I obtain knowledge. When we obtain foreknowledge of contingent claims about the future, it is only by basing beliefs about the future on our knowledge of the past and the laws of nature.

But, if the only way of obtaining foreknowledge of contingent claims about the future that we know of is to obtain such foreknowledge on the basis of one's knowledge of the past and the laws of nature, then we have inductive reason to affirm that the only way to obtain foreknowledge of contingent claims about the future is to obtain such foreknowledge on the basis of one's knowledge of the past and the laws of nature. In other words, inductive reasoning performed on observed cases of foreknowledge reveals that there is good reason to think that every case of foreknowledge of contingent claims about the future is one where such foreknowledge is obtained on the basis of the believer's knowledge of the past and laws of nature. In the same way that our observations of ravens offers inductive support for the claim that all ravens are black, our observation of cases of foreknowledge offers inductive support for the claim that all cases of foreknowledge of contingent claims about the future are ones where such foreknowledge is obtained on the basis of the believer's knowledge of the past and laws of nature.

If, however, we have good reason to affirm that all cases of foreknowledge of contingent claims about the future are ones where such foreknowledge is obtained on the basis of the believer's knowledge of the past and laws of nature, then we have good reason to affirm that if God has foreknowledge of contingent claims about the future, he has this knowledge on the basis of his knowledge of the past and laws of nature. Of course, given that God has exhaustive foreknowledge, it will follow that God has foreknowledge of contingent claims about the future. So, given that God has exhaustive foreknowledge, we have good reason to affirm that God attains this foreknowledge on the basis of his knowledge of the past and laws of nature.

God's knowledge is supposed to be infallible, however. His knowledge must be such that he couldn't have gone wrong in his beliefs. Thus, given that God's beliefs in contingent claims about the future are based on his knowledge of the past and laws of nature, it must be that if the claims God knows about the past and laws of nature are true, then the contingent claims God believes about the future are true as well. It couldn't have been that the past and laws were as God believes and yet the future be different from the way God believes it will be. In other words, the past and laws guarantee that the future will be as it is. The future, including the contingent future, is just a necessary consequence of the past and laws, given that God has infallible and exhaustive foreknowledge. But this is simply to say that given that God has infallible and exhaustive foreknowledge, causal determinism is true. Infallible and exhaustive foreknowledge requires the truth of causal determinism. And this is what we set out to show.

For ease of reference, the foregoing argument is re-presented as follows. The argument is a conditional proof:

(1) God has exhaustive and infallible foreknowledge. (supposition for conditional proof)

(2) God has infallible foreknowledge of contingent claims about the future. (from (1) by definition of exhaustive foreknowledge)

(3) Every case of foreknowledge of contingent claims about the future we know of is a case where this foreknowledge is obtained on the basis of the believer's knowledge of the past and laws of nature. (Premise)

(4) Every case of foreknowledge of contingent claims about the future is a case where this foreknowledge is obtained on the basis of the believer's knowledge of the past and laws of nature. (by induction from 3)

(5) God's infallible foreknowledge of contingent claims about the future is obtained on the basis of God's knowledge of the past and laws of nature. (from (2) and (4))

(6) If God's infallible foreknowledge of contingent claims about the future is obtained on the basis of God's knowledge of the past and laws of nature, then causal determinism is true. (by definition of infallible foreknowledge and definition of causal determinism)

(7) So, causal determinism is true. (from (5) and (6))

(8) So, if God has exhaustive and infallible foreknowledge, then causal determinism is true. (from (1)–(7) by Conditional Proof)

If the argument is cogent, then it shows that we have good reason to think that exhaustive and infallible divine foreknowledge requires the truth of causal determinism. And there is much to say in favor of the argument's cogency. (1) should not be rejected since it is simply a supposition. (2) follows by definition from (1). (3) is a premise that would be very difficult to dispute. (4) is inferred via induction from (3). (5) follows logically from (2) and (4). (6) is true by definition. And (7) and (8) follow logically from previous claims in the argument. Thus, we have a powerful argument in favor of the claim that divine foreknowledge requires the truth of causal determinism. Accordingly, given that it is already dialectically attractive for an advocate of the foreknowledge argument to affirm that the truth of causal determinism would explain the absence of human freedom, she should find the proposal that it is the truth of causal determinism which is both required by infallible divine foreknowledge and explains the absence of human freedom very attractive. Indeed, this proposal is the *best* known proposal concerning that which is both required by divine foreknowledge and explains the absence of human freedom. Thus, if one wishes to pursue the strategic response to the foreknowledge argument I outlined at the beginning of this chapter, she will need to find some response to the foregoing argument.

3. Conclusion

I began this chapter by introducing a strategy of responding to the foreknowledge argument which does not involve denying any of that argument's premises or inferences. The response involves two steps. The first step is to show that we are in a position to know that the foreknowledge argument is sound only if we are in a position to know that there is something which is both required by the existence of divine foreknowledge and which would explain why human beings lack freedom. This step was carried out in Section 1 of this chapter. The second step is to argue that we are not in a position to know that there is something which is both required by the existence of divine foreknowledge and which would explain why human beings lack freedom. The defense of this step was only begun in the present chapter; it must continue for the remainder of the book.

I propose the following two-step defense of claim that we are not in a position to know that there is something which is both required by the existence of divine foreknowledge and which would explain why human beings lack freedom. First, we argue that the very best candidate we know of for such a thing is the truth of causal determinism. Second, we argue that the truth of causal determinism fails to provide us with something we know to be both required by divine foreknowledge and such that it would explain the absence of human freedom. Thus, if there is a something that is both required by divine foreknowledge and that explains the absence of human freedom, it is not a proposal we know of—at best it is one that would need to be developed in the future. Thus, we are not currently in a position to know that there is something which is both required by the existence of divine foreknowledge and which would explain why human beings lack freedom.

In Section 2 of the current chapter I explained why the truth of causal determinism is the best candidate we know of for that which is both required by the existence of divine foreknowledge and which would explain why human beings lack freedom. It is the best candidate for two reasons. First, the main opponents of the foreknowledge argument must grant that *if* causal determinism were true, it would explain the absence of human freedom. Second, there is, as we saw, a powerful argument that divine foreknowledge *does* requires the truth of causal determinism. As no other proposal we know of performs equally well on these scores, the proposal that the truth of causal determinism is both required by the existence of divine foreknowledge and explains why human beings lack freedom is the best proposal we know of.

Not only is the truth of causal determinism the best proposal we know of, however; it is a very good one. Indeed, if the strategic response I am proposing is to be successful, its advocate must find a way to show that the powerful argument of Section 2 of this chapter does not succeed. He must find a way to show that this argument does not put us in a position to know that divine foreknowledge requires the truth of causal determinism. This is the only available option for advocates of this strategy, since an advocate of this strategy by definition must admit that the truth of causal determinism would explain the absence of human freedom. Accordingly, it is precisely toward this task that I will turn in the remainder of the text. My aim will be to show that we are not in a position to know that divine foreknowledge requires the truth of causal determinism. Thus, as the truth of causal determinism is the best candidate we know of for something which is both required by the existence of divine foreknowledge and which would explain why human beings lack freedom, we are not in a position to know that the foreknowledge argument succeeds. After developing the details of this strategy at some length in the next two chapters, I will return to the question of whether the strategy satisfies the three success criteria discussed at the outset of this chapter, arguing that it does.

Foreknowledge and Causal Determinism

The previous chapter sketched a unique strategy which one might employ in order to respond to the foreknowledge argument—a strategy which does not involve disputing any particular premise or inference in the foreknowledge argument. The first step of the strategy is to show that we are in a position to know that the foreknowledge argument is sound only if we are in a position to know that divine foreknowledge requires something which would explain why human beings lack freedom. This step was accomplished in the previous chapter. The second step of the strategy is to argue that we are not in a position to know that divine foreknowledge requires something which would explain why human beings lack freedom. I continue the defense of this step in the present chapter.

The previous chapter began to implement a defense of the second step of the strategy by arguing that the best candidate we know of for that which is both required by divine foreknowledge and which would explain the absence of human freedom is the truth of causal determinism. Thus, we are in a position to know that divine foreknowledge requires something which would explain the absence of human freedom only if we are in a position to know that divine foreknowledge requires the truth of causal determinism. I proposed to defend the claim that we are *not* in a position to know that divine foreknowledge requires the truth of causal determinism, however, by showing that we are not in a position to know that the best argument for the conclusion that divine foreknowledge does require the truth of causal determinism is cogent. The argument I am calling the "best" argument for the conclusion that divine foreknowledge does require the truth of causal determinism is the inductive argument presented in the previous chapter. Thus, my proposal is to complete the second step of the proposed strategy by disputing the cogency of the argument articulated in the previous chapter which attempts to show that divine foreknowledge requires the truth of causal determinism.

This chapter develops two promising strategies for disputing the cogency of the aforementioned inductive argument. Both strategies question the justification of the inductive generalization which figures prominently in that argument. And both strategies significantly parallel strategies theists have pursued in an attempt to dispute the justification of a key inductive generalization in the evidential argument from evil against theism. The first strategy, discussed in Section 1, resembles the strategy used by skeptical theists to respond to the argument from evil against theism. I argue, however, that the strategy employed here escapes several of the negative consequences often thought to follow from skeptical theism. The second strategy, discussed in Section 2, resembles the practice some theists have adopted wherein they tell conciliatory stories with varying epistemic statuses falling short of epistemic justification according to which evils for which there seems not to be a justification are in fact justified. I similarly propose that opponents of the foreknowledge argument tell conciliatory stories with varying epistemic statuses falling short of epistemic justification according to which those claims divine foreknowledge of which seems to require the truth of causal determinism are in fact foreknown by God without the truth of causal determinism. After defending this practice of conciliatory storytelling in this chapter and briefly exploring some extant examples of it, I move on to articulate such a conciliatory story of my own in Chapter 4. One advantage of the story I will articulate is that it does not face the objections thought to render the likelihood of other extant stories very low.

1. Skepticism about ways of knowing

This section begins with a brief discussion of skeptical theist responses to the inductive argument from evil. I then move on to develop a response to the inductive argument of Chapter 2 for the conclusion that divine foreknowledge requires the truth of causal determinism which significantly parallels these skeptical theist responses. I argue, moreover, that the response I develop avoids several of the key difficulties often thought to threaten these skeptical theist approaches to the problem of evil.

We can begin with an argument schema which illustrates the general form which inductive arguments from evil take, as follows:

(1) If theism is true, then every case of evil is a case of evil which God has justifying reasons to permit. (by definition)
(2) E is a case of evil and no reason we know of is a reason which justifies God in permitting E. (premise)
(3) So, E is a case of evil and E is not a case of evil which God has justifying reasons to permit. (by inductive generalization from (3))
(4) So, theism is not true. (from (1) and (3))

Inductive arguments from evil which use this schema differ from one another simply in the selection of the particular evil, or class of evils, E. Some have selected earthquakes,[1] others have selected the death of a fawn in a forest fire,[2] and so on.

There is little room for the theist to challenge arguments with this form. Few theists will deny claim (1), which is supposed to be true by definition of theism. Claim (2) is an empirical claim, which is difficult to deny. (3) is derived through inductive generalization from (2). And (4) follows logically from (1) and (4).

---

[1] See, e.g., Tooley (2008).
[2] Rowe (1979).

Skeptical theists target the inference from (2) to (3). What they find suspicious in the inference of (3) from (2), of course, is not the first conjunct of (3)—that E is an evil. This conjunct is entailed by the first conjunct of (2). Rather, what skeptical theists find suspicious is the inference of the second conjunct of (3) from the second conjunct of (2). As in any inductive generalization, the skeptical theist observes that the inference of the second conjunct of (3) from the second conjunct of (2) involves inferring that a property is possessed by a certain percentage of the members (in this case 100 percent) of an entire population on the basis of that property being possessed by this percentage of members of an observational sample of that population. In this case, the observational sample is all the reasons we know of and the entire population is all the reasons. Because our observational sample of reasons is such that each and every member of it fails to be a reason which justifies God in permitting E, the arguer infers that the entire population of reasons is such that each and every member of it fails to be a reason which justifies God in permitting E. But skeptical theists maintain that inductive generalizations of this sort are not always justified. For example, it would be silly to conclude that because one's observed sample of tiny bacteria was empty (say, because one looked for bacteria with one's naked eye), the entire population of tiny bacteria was empty. Skeptical theists affirm that the inductive generalization from (2) to (3) is among those inductive generalizations which are not justified.

When is one justified or not justified in making such inductive generalizations? This is a matter about which skeptical theists differ. A common proposal is that inductive generalizations of any sort are only justified when certain enabling premises are reasonably believed. Wykstra (1984, 2007),[3] for example, proposes that inferring that an entire population of xs has a property because one's observational sample of xs has it is justified only if it is reasonable to think that were the entire population not to have the property, this would be detectable in one's sample. Bergmann (2001, 2009) proposes that inferring that an entire population of xs has a property because one's observational sample of xs has it is justified only if it is reasonable to think that one's sample is representative. Wykstra and Bergmann both then go on to argue that, in the inference from (2) to (3) seen earlier, their proposed necessary condition on the justification of inductive inferences is not satisfied.

A slightly different approach would be to argue that no enabling premises need to be reasonably believed for an inductive inference to be justified, but that there are certain claims which, *if* reasonably believed, will nonetheless prevent the inference from being justified. One might argue, for example, that inferring that an entire population of xs has a property because one's observational sample of xs has it is not justified if it is reasonable to believe that one's sample of xs is *not* representative. According to this proposal, one needn't hold any beliefs about the representativeness of one's observational sample in order for an inductive inference to be justified; but, if one reasonably believes that one's sample is not representative this will render inductive inferences on the basis of that sample unjustified. It seems to me that some skeptical theists have (perhaps unwittingly) advocated this latter approach, rather than one of

---

[3] McBrayer (2010) is clear about this feature of Bergmann's and Wykstra's proposals.

the two in the previous paragraph. For, they have been concerned with offering reasons for thinking that it is reasonable to think that our sample of justifying reasons for permitting evils is not representative of the entire population of such reasons. In favor of this view, they have argued, for example, that with respect to determining God's reasons, we are rather like a novice chess player who has good reason to think that his sample of reasons for making chess moves is not representative of the reasons that a master chess player has for making chess moves.[4]

Whether of the former sort or the latter sort, skeptical theism has been met with a good deal of resistance, both from theists and from non-theists. Among the most serious concerns facing skeptical theist proposals are that they threaten more widespread skepticism and that they somehow conflict with moral deliberation or moral knowledge. The former charge has been pressed in particular against versions of skeptical theism which require that enabling premises be reasonably believed if inductive inferences are to be justified. Several philosophers have been concerned that, if we adopt this requirement, it will render many cases of inductive reasoning unjustified.[5] The latter charge seems to be directed equally well at both kinds of skeptical theism. If we must remain agnostic about whether there are reasons which would justify God in permitting a certain instance of evil, critics argue that we must remain agnostic about whether there are reasons which justify our permitting it, too. And this has been thought to conflict with our intuitive beliefs about moral knowledge and moral deliberation.[6]

Let us now turn to the inductive argument of Chapter 2 for the claim that divine foreknowledge requires the truth of causal determinism. We can see that there are approaches to responding to this argument which significantly parallel skeptical theist responses to the inductive argument from evil by attending to the key inductive generalization in that argument. That generalization was from claim (3) to claim (4) in that argument, as follows:

(3) Every case of foreknowledge of contingent claims about the future we know
     of is a case where this foreknowledge is obtained on the basis of the believer's
     knowledge of the past and the laws of nature.

(4) So, every case of foreknowledge of contingent claims about the future is a case
     where this foreknowledge is obtained on the basis of the believer's knowledge of
     the past and laws of nature.

Given (4), it follows that if God has knowledge of contingent claims about the future, his knowledge, too, is based on his knowledge of the past and laws of nature. And, since God's knowledge is infallible, this implies that divine foreknowledge requires the truth of causal determinism—the conclusion I wish to avoid.

---

[4] See Alston (1996). Other analogies, chiefly the parent–child analogy, have been advanced as well. See Plantinga (1988). For a clearer example of someone who argues that we have reason to think that our sample is *not* representative, see Sennett (1993).

[5] See McBrayer (2009), which presses this thesis against Wykstra's approach discussed in the text; and, see Wilks (2009), which presses it against Bergmann's approach.

[6] See, e.g., Almeida and Oppy (2003, 2004) and Trakakis (2003).

Here I want to suggest that one promising way of disputing the cogency of the inductive argument from Chapter 2 is to dispute the justification of the inference from (3) to (4) in much the same way that skeptical theists have disputed the inference from (2) to (3) in the argument from evil earlier. In particular, my suggestion is that one argue that the inference from (3) to (4) is an inductive generalization, where it is concluded that an entire population has a property because an observational sample does, but where it is reasonable to believe that our observational sample is *not* representative. Here the sample is cases of foreknowledge of contingent claims about the future that we know of and the population is cases of foreknowledge of contingent claims about the future. Thus, my suggestion is that one argue that it is reasonable to believe that the cases of foreknowledge of contingent claims about the future that we know of are not representative of the total population of cases of foreknowledge of contingent claims about the future.

How could one defend the idea that it is reasonable to believe that our observational sample of cases of foreknowledge of contingent claims about the future is not representative? One might invoke considerations very similar to those invoked by the skeptical theist. For example, our situation with respect to discovering how superior cognitive beings might know the future is analogous to the situation of a chess novice attempting to discern how the chess master knows which move his opponent will make next. Perhaps the strongest reasons here, however, derive from the fact that we have very good inductive reason to think that there are ways of knowing more generally of which we are ignorant.

It is well-known that our sample of ways of knowing has been unrepresentative time and again in the past. There have always been ways of knowing of which we were ignorant which differed significantly from the ways of knowing with which we were acquainted. That bats can know via sonar was something that was discovered, for example. The process of knowing via sonar, as well as its phenomenology, differs significantly from ways of knowing with which (most) humans are familiar. There was a time at which the ways of knowing which we knew of did not include any relevantly like this one. Similarly, it was discovered that savants have incredible epistemic gifts. They exercise epistemic powers which the typical human being simply does not have or cannot exercise. There was a time at which the ways of knowing of which we knew did not include any relevantly like those employed by the savant. And we could go on multiplying examples. The main point here is simple, though: time and again, our sample of ways of knowing has not been representative of the entire population of ways of knowing.

But, if time and again our sample of ways of knowing has not been representative of the entire population of ways of knowing, then there is good reason to think that our current sample of ways of knowing is also not representative of the entire population of ways of knowing. There is good reason to think that all of the ways of knowing that we currently know of are not representative of all of the ways of knowing that there are. And this claim will undercut the justification of the inference from (3) to (4) in the inductive argument of Chapter 2. The fact that each member of our sample of ways of knowing the future is one in which the belief about the future is based on the believer's knowledge of the past and laws of nature does not justify the inference that every member of the entire population of ways of knowing the future is one in which the belief about the future is based on the believer's knowledge of the past and laws of nature. Insofar as we have reason to think that our sample ways of knowing are not representative of all of the ways of knowing, we have reason to doubt that every way of knowing will share a property in common with the ways of knowing that we know of. Thus, insofar as we have reason to think that our sample ways of knowing are not representative of all of the ways of knowing, we have reason to doubt that every way of knowing the future will share a property in common with the ways of knowing the future that we know of.

Initially, one might be concerned that this proposal is no better off than the skeptical theist proposals discussed previously. If there is reason to think that there are ways of knowing of which we are ignorant, then won't this threaten our inductive generalizations and our moral knowledge and deliberation just as much as the skeptical theist views presented earlier? For example, won't the fact that it is reasonable to believe that there are ways of knowing of which we are ignorant give us reason to think that for any population of xs, there is information about that population that is available only through ways of knowing of which we are ignorant and so there is reason to doubt that our sample of xs is representative?

It turns out that the answer here is negative. First, the fact that we have good reason to think that our sample of ways of knowing is not representative can threaten the inductive generalization from (3) to (4) without threatening inductive generalizations more generally. For, the fact that it is reasonable for us to believe that our sample of ways of knowing is not representative will threaten an inductive generalization from a sample of xs to a population of xs only if there is reason to think that ways of knowing of which we are ignorant may well provide access to information about xs which differs from the information provided about xs by the ways of knowing which we know of. In the case of many inductive generalizations, there will not be reason to think that ways of knowing of which we are ignorant may well provide access to information about the population of xs which differs from the information about xs provided by the ways of knowing that we know of. For example, by employing only ways of knowing which I know of, I gather that my observational sample of human beings is such that each member of that sample is less than twelve feet tall. Now, I have reason to think that there are ways of knowing of which I am ignorant. But, I don't have reason to think that any of these ways of knowing may well reveal information about the population of human beings which will differ from the information about human beings which has been provided by my sample ways of knowing. This is because I have reason to think that my sample ways of knowing are excellent ways of obtaining information about the height of human beings. Thus, in this case, the fact that I have reason to think that there are ways of knowing of which I am ignorant will not show that drawing my inductive generalization is unjustified. Arguably, however, I do have reason to think that ways of knowing of which I am ignorant may well provide information about ways of knowing the future which is not provided by my sample ways of knowing. This is because, time and again, my information about ways of knowing provided through my sample ways of knowing has been unrepresentative. Thus, the fact that I have reason to think that there are ways of knowing of which I am ignorant threatens the inference from (3) to (4) without threatening inductive generalizations more generally.

For similar reasons we can see that the present proposal will not, by itself, undermine our moral knowledge or deliberation, either. In accordance with the previous paragraph, the fact that we have good reason for thinking that there are ways of knowing of which we are ignorant will undermine an inference from <every reason we know of is not a justifying reason> to <there are no justifying reasons> only if we have reason to think that ways of knowing of which we are ignorant may well provide access to information about reasons which differs from that which is provided by our sample ways of knowing. We will not have reason to think that they will do so if we have reason to think that our ways of obtaining information about reasons are excellent ways of obtaining information about reasons. Whether our ways of knowing about reasons are excellent ways of knowing about reasons is a matter of some controversy.[7] Skeptical theists tend to claim that they are not. But, the present proposal does not have any implications about how to resolve this controversy. And, so, it does not on its own have the implication that we should remain agnostic about whether there are justifying reasons for our permitting evils. On its own, it will not conflict with what we intuitively believe about moral knowledge and deliberation.

Given the interest philosophers have taken in skeptical theism and the similarity between the present strategy and skeptical theism, I hope that the present strategy will attract attention from philosophers working on the topic of freedom and foreknowledge. Further, given that the present proposal is less threatened by those objections typically offered to skeptical theist views, I think we have even more motivation to give it a hearing. Thus, while I have only scratched the surface of this proposal here, I hope that my introducing it here will ignite some discussion of its promise in future literature.

There is certainly more to say in order to determine the extent to which a strategy like that proposed here will successfully challenge the inductive argument of Chapter 2 for the conclusion that divine foreknowledge requires the truth of causal determinism. In particular, we must attend carefully to questions such as the following. How have our sample ways of knowing been unrepresentative in the past? Inhowfar do the ways in which they have been unrepresentative give us reason to think that our present sample is unrepresentative with respect to the mechanics whereby contingent claims about the future are known? Are there any reasons for thinking that, at least with respect to the ways whereby contingent claims about the future can be known, our current sample *is* representative? I will not address these questions further here. For, I wish to move on to discuss and implement a second strategy for responding to the argument of Chapter 2. I simply note that future discussion of the present proposed strategy will need to attend carefully to these questions. I hope that this text's introduction of this proposal will spark some conversation about these issues in the near future.

---

[7] Compare, for example, the different perspectives represented in Tooley (1991), Sennett (1993) and Bergmann (2009).

2. Conciliatory stories

In this section, I will introduce a second strategy for disputing the inference from (3) to (4) in the inductive argument from Chapter 2. The strategy involves telling conciliatory stories of varying epistemic statuses falling short of epistemic justification in a way that mimics a strategy employed by some theists in their response to the inductive argument from evil. I will begin by explaining how the strategy of telling conciliatory stories is employed by some theists in response to the problem of evil, and I will then explain how a similar strategy may be adopted by an opponent of the foreknowledge argument in order to respond to the inductive argument of Chapter 2. In my explanation of how the strategy is implemented in the context of the problem of evil, I follow closely the work of Trent Dougherty and Alexander Pruss (forthcoming).

Recall the argument schema introduced earlier, which is employed by many versions of the inductive argument from evil:

(1) If theism is true, then every case of evil is a case of evil which God has justifying reasons to permit. (by definition)
(2) E is a case of evil and no reason we know of is a reason which justifies God in permitting E. (premise)
(3) So, E is a case of evil and E is not a case of evil which God has justifying reasons to permit. (by inductive generalization from (3))
(4) So, theism is not true. (from (1) and (3))

The practice of telling conciliatory stories is aimed at disputing the strength of the inference from (2) to (3). In particular, it is aimed at disputing the inference of the second conjunct of (3) from the second conjunct of (2). Thus, the aim of the strategy is to show that the fact that no reason we know of is a reason which justifies God in permitting an evil E does not provide us with very good reason for thinking that there is no reason which justifies God in permitting E.

In order to accomplish this aim, the strategy proposes that the theist tell conciliatory stories. These are stories in which God permits E and has justifying reasons for doing so where the stories in question have varying epistemic statuses falling short of epistemic justification. That the stories fall short of being fully justified is what shows that the present strategy is *not* a strategy of denying (2). It is not a strategy of arguing that there *is* some reason we know of that in fact justifies God in permitting E. Rather, the strategy is to propose stories we are not justified in believing in which God does have reasons for permitting E, and to argue that the presence of such stories significantly weakens the inference of (3) from (2).

One immediately wonders: if we *aren't* justified in believing the stories, then how can they show that the inference from (2) to (3) is unjustified? The answer lies in seeing the problem of evil as a special case of the problem of anomaly.

A theory faces an anomaly when it implies a universal generalization, $\forall x(Fx \to Gx)$, but there is a y such that it seems that $Fy \ \& \sim Gy$. The anomaly in such a case is y. And, the problem of anomaly is the problem of explaining how it can be rational for an advocate of the theory in question to maintain her theory in light of y.

Dougherty and Pruss explain that the disconfirmation of a theory provided by an anomaly is a matter of degree. Specifically, they propose that the degree of disconfirmation of a theory T provided by an anomaly x can be captured by the Bayes' Factor, as follows:

$$Pr(T/x) = Pr(x/{\sim}T)/Pr(x/T).$$

That is, the likelihood of a theory given an anomaly is equal to the likelihood of the anomaly given that the theory is false divided by the likelihood of the anomaly given that the theory is true. In other words, an anomaly disconfirms a theory to the extent that the anomaly is more likely without the theory than with it.

Dougherty and Pruss draw several important lessons from this account of the degree to which an anomaly disconfirms a theory. One lesson is that it can be rational to maintain a theory in the face of an anomaly without developing any sort of account of how to explain away the anomaly. This is because, especially in those cases where a theory generates particularly wide-ranging universal generalizations, it is to be expected that there will be anomalies for the theory. Thus, the number for $Pr(x/T)$ may not be low. The higher this number is, the lower will be the degree to which the anomaly disconfirms the theory.

This latter fact is what helps to explain the value of conciliatory stories as well. These stories will be stories according to which T is true and x occurs—stories according to which the theory in question is true and the anomaly occurs. Thus, to the extent that such theories are likely, they show that the likelihood of the anomaly given the theory may be higher than expected. And this in turn shows that the degree to which the anomaly disconfirms the theory may not be as high as expected. Thus, one strategy for responding to the problem of anomaly is to tell such conciliatory stories. The stories may vary in epistemic status. Some may be merely-possibly-so stories, others consistent-with-what-we-know stories, others not-unlikely stories, others maybe-so stories, and others may-very-well-be stories. Though none are very likely stories, even one may-very-well-be story may show that the anomaly in question does not significantly disconfirm the theory. And several disjoined not-unlikely stories will have the same effect. Thus, one way for an advocate of a theory to respond to an anomaly is to tell such conciliatory stories.

The application to the problem of evil is straightforward. For, the argument schema presented earlier highlights that the problem of evil is an argument in which an anomaly is urged as a challenge to theism. Premise (1) tells us that theism implies a certain universal generalization. And, premise (2) claims that there is an anomaly facing theism, because there is an example which seems to be a counterexample to this universal generalization. Dougherty and Pruss will claim that the extent to which this proposed anomaly threatens theism—and so the extent to which it confirms (3)—will depend upon the extent to which the anomaly is expectable given theism. The more likely the anomaly is given theism, the less the anomaly will threaten theism. And one way to show that the anomaly is not unlikely given theism is to tell conciliatory stories, as many who have responded to the argument from evil have done. These will be stories where God has justifying reasons for permitting the evil in question, where these stories range in epistemic status from merely-possibly-so, to consistent-with-what-we-know to not-unlikely, to maybe-so to may-very-well-be.

What I wish to propose here is that the opponent of the foreknowledge argument responds to the foreknowledge argument in a similar fashion. The opponent of the foreknowledge argument advocates a classical theory of divine omniscience which generates the wide-ranging universal generalization that every true proposition p is infallibly foreknown by God. The advocate of the foreknowledge argument challenges this theory by urging an anomaly against it. She proposes that <Elizabeth sings a love sonnet to John at t_{100}> is a true proposition but that it is not infallibly foreknown by God. As we saw in Chapter 2, we are in a position to know that her argument is sound only if we are in a position to know that the following inference is inductively strong:

(3) Every case of foreknowledge of contingent claims about the future we know of is a case where this foreknowledge is obtained on the basis of the believer's knowledge of the past and laws of nature.

(4) So, every case of foreknowledge of contingent claims about the future is a case where this foreknowledge is obtained on the basis of the believer's knowledge of the past and laws of nature.

My proposal here is that the opponent of the foreknowledge argument respond to this objection to her theory by using conciliatory stories to cast doubt on the inference from (3) to (4). The approach is to tell stories with a range of epistemic statuses falling short of epistemic justification in which some cases of foreknowledge of contingent claims about the future are not known on the basis of the believer's knowledge of the past and the laws. More specifically, they will be stories where God infallibly foreknows <Elizabeth sings a love sonnet to John at t_{100}> but not in a way that requires the truth of causal determinism.

To see more clearly the close parallel between Dougherty's and Pruss's response to the problem of evil and the response that I am advocating here to the foreknowledge argument, it is helpful to recast the objection to the classical theory of divine omniscience presented by the foreknowledge argument more compactly as follows:

(5) If the classical theory of divine omniscience is true, then every true proposition is infallibly foreknown by God.

(6) But, <Elizabeth sings a love sonnet to John at t_{100}> is true and no way of knowing the future we know of is a way whereby God infallibly foreknows <Elizabeth sings a love sonnet to John at t_{100}>.

(7) So, <Elizabeth sings a love sonnet to John at t_{100}> is true and God does not infallibly foreknow <Elizabeth sings a love sonnet to John at t_{100}>.

(8) So, the classical theory of divine omniscience is not true.

In this argument, (5) is supposed to be true by definition. The left conjunct of (6) is dialectically innocent, since the advocate of the classical theory of divine omniscience accepts it. The right conjunct of (6) is an empirical claim which should be no less plausible than the right conjunct in premise (3) from Chapter 2. After all, the reason why no way of knowing the future we know of is a way whereby God infallibly foreknows <Elizabeth sings a love sonnet to John at t_{100}> is that all of the ways of knowing the future we know of are ways wherein the believer bases his belief about the future on his knowledge of the past and laws of nature, and this cannot be how God infallibly foreknows <Elizabeth sings a love sonnet to John at t_{100}>, since it would require the truth of causal determinism. As we will see momentarily, the inference from (6) to (7) is just as strong as the inference from (3) to (4) in the argument of Chapter 2. And, conclusion (8) follows by *modus tollens* from (5) and (7). Structurally, the argument from (5) to (8) exactly parallels the argument schema of the inductive problem of evil in (1)–(4) presented earlier.

The inference from (6) to (7) is key. I propose here that the advocate of the foreknowledge argument must think that this inference is just as strong as the inference from (3) to (4) in the argument of Chapter 2. In the inference from (3) to (4) in the argument of Chapter 2, the advocate of the foreknowledge argument proposes that because every way of knowing the future we know of is a way wherein the believer holds her belief on the basis of her knowledge of the past and laws of nature, every way of knowing the future is a way wherein the believer holds her belief on the basis of her knowledge of the past and laws of nature. However, the advocate of the foreknowledge argument who endorses the argument of Chapter 2 will think that no way of knowing the future wherein the believer bases her belief on her knowledge of the past and laws of nature is a way whereby God infallibly foreknows <Elizabeth sings a love sonnet to John at t_{100}>. This is because, if God infallibly foreknew <Elizabeth sings a love sonnet to John at t_{100}> in such a way, this would require the truth of causal determinism, which would conflict with Elizabeth's singing at t_{100} being done freely. Thus, the advocate of the foreknowledge argument who endorses the argument of Chapter 2 will think that <every way of foreknowing contingent propositions about the future we know of is a way wherein the believer bases her belief on her knowledge of the past and laws of nature> entails <no way of knowing the future we know of is a way whereby God infallibly foreknows <Elizabeth sings a love sonnet to John at t_{100}>>; and she will think that <every way of foreknowing contingent propositions about the future is a way wherein the believer bases her belief on her knowledge of the past and laws of nature> entails <no way of knowing the future is a way whereby God infallibly foreknows <Elizabeth sings a love sonnet to John at t_{100}>>. In other words, she will think that the right conjunct of (3) entails the right conjunct of (6) and that the right conjunct of (4) entails the right conjunct of (7). Further, she thinks that the right conjunct of (6) is true because the right conjunct of (3) is true. No way of knowing the future we know of is a way whereby God infallibly foreknows <Elizabeth sings a love sonnet to John at t_{100}>, because every way of knowing the future we know of is a way wherein the believer bases her belief on her knowledge of the past and laws of nature. But, then, it will follow that if the right conjunct of (3) strongly inductively supports the right conjunct of (4), the right conjunct of (6) equally strongly inductively supports the right conjunct of (7). Thus, the advocate of the foreknowledge argument who endorses the argument of Chapter 2 should think that the inference from (6) to (7) is just as strong as the inference from (3) to (4) in the argument of Chapter 2.

The success of the foreknowledge argument depends upon the cogency of the argument from (5) to (8) shown earlier. This is because, as we saw in Chapter 2, we are in a position to know that the foreknowledge argument is sound only if we are in a position to know that the argument of Chapter 2 is cogent, and, as we have just seen here, if the argument of Chapter 2 is cogent, then so is the argument from (5) to (8). Indeed, we might think of the argument from (5) to (8) as recasting the foreknowledge argument more compactly. Accordingly, if the opponent of the foreknowledge argument can successfully dispute the cogency of the argument from (5) to (8), she will have challenged the foreknowledge argument. This is because, by successfully disputing the cogency of the argument from (5) to (8), she successfully disputes the cogency of the argument of Chapter 2, and thereby shows that we are not in a position to know that the foreknowledge argument is sound. The remainder of this section proposes a method the opponent of the foreknowledge argument can use to dispute the cogency of (5)–(8) and thereby a method she can use to dispute the soundness of the foreknowledge argument.

A promising approach to disputing the cogency of (5)–(8) involves adopting the practice proposed by Dougherty and Pruss of telling conciliatory stories. Notice again the structural parallel between (5)–(8) and (1)–(4) from earlier in the present chapter. In each case, an anomaly is brought forth to challenge a theory. The anomaly consists in a proposed counterexample or group of counterexamples to a universal generalization entailed by the theory. While the theory entails some universal generalization, $\forall x(Fx \rightarrow Gx)$, the anomaly, it is argued, is an example of some y which is F but not G. In each case, the claim that the example in question is something that is an F but not a G is defended through the use of an inductive generalization. In the argument from evil schema, the anomaly is an example of an evil which is such that no reason we know of is a reason justifies God in permitting it. It is inferred on this basis that the evil is one which is such that there is no reason which justifies God in permitting it. In the compact recasting of the foreknowledge argument, the anomaly is an example of a true proposition which is such that no way of knowing the future we know of is a way whereby this proposition is infallibly foreknown by God. It is concluded on this basis that the anomaly is an example of a true proposition such that no way of knowing the future is a way that God infallibly foreknows this proposition. In each case, however, Dougherty's and Pruss's lesson about the degree of disconfirmation that the anomaly provides for a theory holds: the anomaly y disconfirms the theory T to the degree that the anomaly is more likely given the falsity of the theory than given the truth of the theory. In the schematic argument from evil, the degree to which the anomalous evil E disconfirms theism is exactly Pr(E/theism is false)/Pr(E/theism is true). Likewise, in the compact recasting of the foreknowledge argument, the degree to which the anomalous proposition <Elizabeth sings a love sonnet to John at t_{100}>

disconfirms the classical theory of divine omniscience is exactly $\Pr(<$Elizabeth sings a love sonnet to John at $t_{100}>$ is true/the classical theory of divine omniscience is false)/ $\Pr(<$Elizabeth sings a love sonnet to John at $t_{100}>$ is true/the classical theory of divine omniscience is true). In the former case, the practice of telling conciliatory stories involves telling stories according to which E occurs and theism is true. These stories of varying epistemic statuses falling short of epistemic justification show that the degree to which E disconfirms theism is not very high by showing that $\Pr(E/\text{theism is true})$ is higher than one might have thought without the stories. Similarly, in the latter case, the practice of telling conciliatory stories involves telling stories according to which $<$Elizabeth sings a love sonnet to John at $t_{100}>$ is true, and the classical theory of divine omniscience is true. These stories of varying epistemic statuses falling short of epistemic justification show that the degree to which the truth of $<$Elizabeth sings a love sonnet to John at $t_{100}>$ disconfirms the classical theory of divine cognitive perfection is not very high by showing that $\Pr(<$Elizabeth sings a love sonnet to John at $t_{100}>$ is true/the classical theory of divine cognitive perfection is true) is higher than one might have though independent of the stories.

The practice of telling conciliatory stories will of course be more effective the higher the epistemic status of these stories. As we saw earlier, conciliatory stories can be effective by themselves or effective when disjoined. For a lone conciliatory story to be effective, it needs to have a fairly high epistemic status, though not one reaching the level of epistemic justification. When we have a disjunction of conciliatory stories, it can be effective even if none of its members reached a high epistemic status on its own.

The purpose of the present section has simply been to explain how an opponent of the foreknowledge argument might adopt the practice of telling conciliatory stories in order to challenge the foreknowledge argument. She can do so by telling stories of varying epistemic statuses falling short of epistemic justification according to which $<$Elizabeth sings a love sonnet to John at $t_{100}>$ is true and the classical theory of divine omniscience is true. To the extent that she is able to tell either one such story with a fairly high epistemic status or several such stories with lower epistemic statuses, she will have shown that the degree of disconfirmation which the anomalous proposition $<$Elizabeth sings a love sonnet to John at $t_{100}>$ provides against her theory is not so high as we might have expected independent of these stories. If the degree of disconfirmation is not very high, then the inference from (6) to (7) earlier will not be strong. And if it is not strong, then we are not in a position to know that the foreknowledge argument is sound.

3. Extant conciliatory stories

In the contemporary literature on providence and foreknowledge, it is a standard assumption that there are only two stories, or models, of providence and foreknowledge according to which God has *complete* foreknowledge—where God knows every proposition which has been, is, or will be true.[8] The two models are the Theological Determinist model and the Molinist model. After briefly presenting these theories here and explaining some of their major shortcomings, I show that there is logical space for more stories, or models, of complete foreknowledge. The story I will propose in Chapter 4 fits into this vacant logical space, and I will argue that it overcomes some of the major shortcomings of the Theological Determinist and Molinist models.

It will be helpful to begin an explanation of Theological Determinism and Molinism by considering what they have in common. As Jonathan Kvanvig (2013) points out, both theories share three structural features in common. They each assume a particular background theory about the nature of God according to which God's decisions are complete and immutable; they each specify certain creative and miraculous decisions God makes; and they each employ some sort of conditionals which have in their antecedents information about the creative and miraculous decisions God makes and have in their consequents information about the entire remainder of history. According to the first feature, each theory will rule out God's changing the laws of nature mid-stream, his deciding to intervene miraculously and then changing his mind, and his having gaps about what he intends for creation. The second feature specifies how God decides to set up the initial conditions of creation, and how he decides to intervene miraculously in the course of history. And, the third feature specifies conditionals to be used by God for discerning what will occur in the remainder of history, given his fixed creative and miraculous decisions. Where Theological Determinism and Molinism part company is in which precise creative decisions they claim are made by God and which conditionals God employs to discern what will unfold in the course of history.

The Theological Determinist is keen to emphasize that God's creative decisions include his decisions to establish certain initial conditions for the universe and his decisions to establish the laws of nature governing the universe (as well as any miraculous interventions). The Theological Determinist then proposes that God discerns what will unfold in the remainder of history by employing his knowledge of necessarily true conditionals, specifying what will unfold in the course of history given these initial conditions and laws (and any miraculous interventions). According to the Theological Determinist, it is necessarily the case that if the universe has the initial conditions and the laws that it has (and if God has decided in the way that he has whether and how to miraculously intervene), then it will have the history that it has. In other words, barring miraculous divine intervention, the past and the laws uniquely determine the future.

As such, it would appear that the Theological Determinist simply accepts the truth of causal determinism and employs its truth in her explanation of how God achieves

---

[8] For a salient example, consider Thomas Flint's (2011) chastisement of William Hasker: "I think our conversations should take place with the understanding that there are *three* serious competitors for our support, not just (as Hasker implies in his opening paragraph) two." The three competitors here are Molinism, Theological Determinism (which Hasker had overlooked), and Open Theism. Of course, only the former two models permit complete foreknowledge.

foreknowledge. For, causal determinism is typically thought to claim nothing other than that the past and the laws uniquely determine the future. It is only by virtue, then, of the truth of causal determinism that the Theological Determinist has offered us a story according to which God can know <Elizabeth sings a love sonnet to John at t_{100}> infallibly. Thus, the theological determinist arguably does not offer a story according to which God has infallible foreknowledge but causal determinism is false. One might wonder, then, whether her story could be of any use to the opponent of the foreknowledge argument who believes that human freedom is incompatible with the truth of causal determinism.

As it turns out, the Theological Determinist story is of some minimal utility for such an incompatibilist as a conciliatory story, despite its rather bald acceptance and employment of the truth of causal determinism. The reason for this is that the typical incompatibilist, while she is confident that human freedom requires the absence of causal determinism, will nonetheless think that it is epistemically possible that human freedom and causal determinism are compatible. To assign artificial numerical values, it is not difficult to imagine incompatibilists who place a credence of, say, .9 in incompatibilism, and a credence of .1 in compatibilism. For such an incompatibilist, Theological Determinism may constitute a conciliatory story of a weak epistemic status. For, in her eyes, it is a story of a weak epistemic status falling far short of epistemic justification according to which <Elizabeth sings a love sonnet to John at t_{100}> is true and the classical theory of divine cognitive perfection is true. The story is one she disbelieves, and by itself it will not show that the anomalous proposition <Elizabeth sings a love sonnet to John at t_{100}> does not disconfirm the classical theory of divine cognitive perfection sufficiently to put us in a position to know that it is false. But, and this is the real lesson here, the Theological Determinist story can nonetheless be disjoined with other conciliatory stories so that the incompatibilist might have a disjunctive conciliatory story which *does* show that <Elizabeth sings a love sonnet to John at t_{100}> does not disconfirm the classical theory of divine cognitive perfection sufficiently to put us in a position to know that it is false.

While the Theological Determinist story could be disjoined in this way with other conciliatory stories, the main difficulty facing the Theological Determinist story— the difficulty on account of which it has only a very low epistemic status for the incompatibilist—is obviously its assumption of the truth of causal determinism. If the committed incompatibilist is to disjoin this theory with others to form a disjunctive conciliatory story strong enough to dispute the cogency of the argument of (5)–(8) earlier, she will have to disjoin it with other stories which do not require the truth of causal determinism. The story I will offer in the next chapter, I argue, is one such story.

But perhaps it is not the only such story. Indeed, the Molinist claims that her model for understanding the mechanics of divine providence and foreknowledge is one that does not require the truth of causal determinism, either. In her story, God's knowledge of necessarily true conditionals concerning what will happen (absent miraculous divine intervention) given the initial conditions of the universe and laws of nature does not yield a complete knowledge of history. In particular, God does not know what free creatures will do on the basis of these necessarily true conditionals. Instead,

God knows what free creatures will do on the basis of his knowledge of *subjunctive* conditionals that specify what any free creature S would do in any circumstances C. Because God knows what any creature S would do in any circumstances C, and because God knows which circumstances each free creature will face, God can know infallibly what each free creature will do throughout the entirety of history. In particular, he can know <Elizabeth sings a love sonnet to John at t_{100}> on the basis of his knowledge of subjunctive conditionals specifying what Elizabeth would do in every circumstance she might encounter, together with his knowledge of the circumstances she will encounter. Thus, the Molinist parts company with the Theological Determinist primarily with respect to the third feature presented earlier—which sorts of conditionals she says are employed by God in order to discern how history will unfold. For the Theological Determinist, it is only strict conditionals; for the Molinist it is both strict conditionals and subjunctive conditionals concerning what free creatures would do.

The Molinist story is arguably one which does not require the truth of causal determinism. For, according to this story, it is not the case that the past and laws of nature uniquely determine the future. There are, after all, free actions which according to this story are not infallibly knowable on this view on the basis of one's knowledge of the past and laws.[9] Thus, this conciliatory story arguably will not face the same difficulty from the perspective of an incompatibilist as that faced by the Theological Determinism story. There is some promise, then, that it might be disjoined with the Theological Determinism story to form a disjunctive conciliatory story of considerably higher epistemic status than that of the Theological Determinism story taken by itself.

Unfortunately, significant difficulties plague the Molinist story rendering its epistemic status still very low in the eyes of many, independently of whether or not it requires the truth of causal determinism. Here I discuss only one such difficulty which has been a very important one: the grounding objection. The advocate of this objection urges that because the relevant subjunctive conditionals are not necessarily true but are instead contingently true, they must have some grounding in reality. But, the best candidates for what there might be in reality to ground these conditionals either will conflict with the Molinist's story of God's being able to use these conditionals to achieve foreknowledge of creaturely actions, or they will conflict with the Molinist's commitment to incompatibilism. The reason for this is that the best candidates for that which grounds the truth of these conditionals will be something about the divine will or something about creaturely acts. For example, it might be that God somehow is able to will it to be the case that were Elizabeth to face circumstances C, she would sing a love sonnet to John. Or, it might be that if Elizabeth in fact does sing a love sonnet to John in C, then this very act grounds the truth of the claim that were Elizabeth to face circumstances C, she would sing a love sonnet to John. But, it is unclear how the divine will could ground these conditionals; and, even if it did, one worries that its doing so would render human actions unfree, since they would seem to be brought about by some sort of divine manipulation, which incompatibilists will think undermines

---

[9]   The argument that Molinism does not require the truth of causal determinism, I believe, is considerably more complicated than is typically appreciated. See my discussion in the next chapter.

freedom. On the other hand, if the subjunctive conditionals in question are grounded in creaturely acts, then it seems God could not use them to know what creatures will do, since in order to know them he will already have to know what creatures will do. The Molinist, then, faces a very difficult question about how the subjunctive conditionals which play such an important role in her story can be grounded in a way that does not undermine a crucial element of her story.

In light of this objection to Molinism, many will find the Molinist story to be of a very low epistemic status. As such, even if Molinism does not require the truth of causal determinism, disjoining it with Theological Determinism may not result in a disjunctive conciliatory story which will challenge the ability of the anomalous proposition <Elizabeth sings a love sonnet to John at t_{100}>, to put us in a position to know that the classical theory of divine omniscience is false.

If Theological Determinism and Molinism are the only options for incompatibilists who wished to make use of conciliatory stories in order to respond to the argument of (5)–(8) presented earlier, then these incompatibilists would be in significant trouble. And, as I said before, it is standardly assumed that these *are* the only options. But, thankfully, this standard assumption is wrong. There are more positions available in logical space than Theological Determinism and Molinism for those who wish to employ conciliatory stories to challenge the argument from (5)–(8).

To see why this is so, we need only return to Kvanvig's construal of the structural features shared by Theological Determinism and Molinism. These moving parts were, again, a background theory concerning the completeness and immutability of divine decisions, claims concerning the content of divine creative and miraculous decisions, and conditionals of deliberation taking as their antecedents the contents of divine creative and miraculous decisions and as their consequents the remainder of the history of the world. There is logical space to develop alternatives to Theological Determinism and Molinism here because there is room for alternative proposals concerning the content of the divine creative and miraculous decisions, the content of the conditionals of deliberation, and even the kinds of conditionals employed by the theory. Kvanvig (2011), for his part, proposes an alternative theory which employs a different kind of conditional than either strict conditionals or subjunctive conditionals: epistemic conditionals. Importantly, these epistemic conditionals are grounded in that they are explained by the truth of necessarily true epistemic conditionals like those advocated by Roderick Chisholm (1977). While I do not have the space to explore Kvanvig's proposal in greater detail here, I do recommend it as a view which might be profitably disjoined with Theological Determinism, Molinism, and the conciliatory story I will develop in Part II of this text to form a disjunctive conciliatory story powerful enough to show that the anomalous proposition <Elizabeth sings a love sonnet to John at t_{100}> does not put us in a position to know that the classical theory of divine omniscience is false.

My own approach will not involve proposing that we use a different kind of conditional for the conditionals of deliberation, but it will involve proposing that we use strict conditionals with antecedents having a content which differs from that of the conditionals employed by the theological determinist. Since the conditionals I will use will be strict conditionals, they too will not face the objection that they are not properly grounded. And, as I will argue in detail in Chapters 4 and 5, since their contents differ significantly from the contents of the conditionals employed by the theological determinist, they will not face the objection that they require the truth of causal determinism either.

4. Conclusion

In this chapter, I proposed two ways in which the advocate of the strategy I proposed in Chapter 2 for responding to the foreknowledge argument might complete her defense of that strategy. The strategy involves arguing that we are in a position to know that the foreknowledge argument is sound only if we are in a position to know that divine foreknowledge requires the truth of causal determinism, but that we are not in a position to know that divine foreknowledge requires the truth of causal determinism. My focus in this chapter was on defending the claim that we are not in a position to know that divine foreknowledge requires the truth of causal determinism. I proposed that the opponent of the foreknowledge argument defend this claim by showing that the best argument in favor of it is not cogent. And, I developed two ways of disputing the cogency of that argument—one way which involves defending a view akin to skeptical theism and one way which involves articulating conciliatory stories. I continue my defense of the conciliatory story approach in the remainder of the text by developing a conciliatory story with a higher epistemic status than other canonical conciliatory stories, such as Theological Determinism and Molinism.

Part Two

A Time-ordering Account of
Foreknowledge and Providence

4

Time-ordering and Foreknowledge[1]

In Part I, my aim was to explain how a committed incompatibilist might pursue a general strategy of responding to the foreknowledge argument where this strategy did not involve denying one of that argument's premises or inferences. The proposed strategy involves two steps. The first step is to argue that we are in a position to know that the foreknowledge argument is sound only if we are in a position to know that infallible divine foreknowledge requires the truth of causal determinism. I defended this step in Chapter 2. The second step is to argue that we are not in a position to know that infallible divine foreknowledge requires the truth of causal determinism. I proposed a general strategy whereby the defense of this step might be carried out in Chapter 3. Part II of this text is concerned with making a contribution toward implementing that general strategy.

In Chapter 3, the general strategy I proposed involved arguing that we are not in a position to know that infallible divine foreknowledge requires the truth of causal determinism by challenging a key inductive inference in the best available argument for the claim that divine foreknowledge *does* require the truth of causal determinism. That inductive inference proceeded from the claim that *no way of knowing the future we know of is a way whereby God infallibly foreknows <Elizabeth sings a love sonnet to John at t_{100}>* to the claim that *there is no way whereby God infallibly foreknows <Elizabeth sings a love sonnet to John at t_{100}>*. One of the ways I proposed for the incompatibilist to challenge that inductive inference was by telling conciliatory stories. In order to be employed by the incompatibilist to challenge the inference in question, these stories must be stories of varying epistemic statuses falling short of epistemic justification according to which God has infallible and exhaustive foreknowledge but his attaining this foreknowledge does not require the truth of causal determinism. While the advocate of the strategy I proposed will not claim that any of these stories is one that we know to be true—and so she will not claim that the way of knowing the future employed in it is a way *we know of* whereby God or anyone else knows the future—what she insists is that the not-insignificant epistemic possibility of such stories undercuts the justification of the key inductive generalization highlighted earlier. While we do not know of any ways of knowing the future whereby God infallibly foreknows the proposition in question, what these stories show is that there is a not-insignificant epistemic possibility that

---

[1] I first presented the time-ordering account of foreknowledge in (Byerly forthcoming). The material here is substantially updated and revised, however.

there are such ways. Whether there is just one story or a disjunction of several stories, they can be employed by the incompatibilist to challenge the inductive inference in question to the extent that they exceed a not-very-low epistemic status given theism.

I said that my aim in Part II of this text is to make a contribution toward implementing the general strategy of Part I. I aim to do so by articulating a conciliatory story of the sort just described and arguing that its epistemic status is not very low given theism. According to the conciliatory story I propose here, God achieves exhaustive and infallible foreknowledge through time-ordering.

The presentation of my story in this chapter takes place in two stages. First, I begin in Section 1 by articulating a story according to which God achieves exhaustive and infallible foreknowledge via time-ordering. I show that none of the central elements of the story are very unlikely given theism. Then, in Section 2 I argue that the story is one which does not require causal determinism. If the argument is successful, then the story constitutes a conciliatory story of the sort described earlier, since it is one where God attains exhaustive and infallible foreknowledge without causal determinism which is such that its epistemic status is not very low given theism.

1. Foreknowledge through time-ordering

In this section, I articulate a story according to which God achieves infallible and exhaustive foreknowledge through time-ordering. I argue that the proposed mechanics for divine foreknowledge is not very unlikely given theism. In the next section, I argue that the story does not require the truth of causal determinism.

I'll offer a brief description of the story in this paragraph and then unpack its key conceptual elements in the paragraphs that follow. According to the story, God has infallible foreknowledge by virtue of his self-knowledge, his knowledge of the times, and his infallibly competent deductive powers. God begins with the knowledge of every possible time. God then wills for some of these times to be ordered in a particular way so as to constitute the history of the actual world. By virtue of his self-awareness he knows that he wills this. His willing that the times be ordered in such-and-such a way entails that the times *are* ordered in such-and-such a way, since he is omnipotent. And God knows that he is omnipotent, too, so he deduces that the times are ordered in such-and-such a way. Finally, the times being ordered in such-and-such a way entails everything which occurs in the history of the world, including everything which occurs at every future time. Since God knows this, too, he can competently deduce what will happen at every time, including the future times. Indeed, he can know infallibly what will happen at every time, since his evidence entails everything that happens at every time. Since knowing infallibly everything that ever happens suffices for knowing infallibly every truth, God is classically omniscient.

I'll now say more about some important elements of the story, beginning with the metaphysical elements, and argue that none of these elements is unlikely given theism. Start with the times. The story I tell takes times seriously. There really are times, according to my story. Talk of times is not made true only by entities none of which are times; rather, at least some of it is made true by times. That there are times is not a view without motivation. For, times enable us to explain the nature of certain entities and they help us carefully define views. For example, events are commonly defined in terms of times. An event e is an exemplification of a property by an object at a *time*.[2] And many views, such as views about personal identity and about causal determinism (as we shall see in Section 2 later) are defined with explicit reference to times. Thus, taking times seriously should not by itself make my story very unlikely.

Given that there are times, *what* are they? As I will develop my story here, it borrows from a view with an impressive pedigree in the philosophy of time according to which times are some sort of maximal or nearly maximal abstract representational object.[3] This view contrasts with views according to which times are concrete entities. I am not entirely persuaded that the story I describe here could not be re-told as a story employing concrete times. But it is easier to see how the story would go for a friend of abstract times; so I shall start there.

According to my story, times are nearly maximal, consistent propositions.[4] A maximal proposition is a proposition which, for every proposition p, includes either p or not-p as a conjunct. The times in my story needn't *quite* be maximal. They may include, for every proposition p *except for propositions about relations between times*, either p or not-p as a conjunct.[5] This is their essential nature, anyway. What makes a time the particular time that it is has to do only with propositions it includes, which don't say anything about that time's relation to other times. But, contingently, a time may include propositions about which other times it is related to. Thus, the times in my theory say everything about what is going on at those times except for how other times are related to those times, so long as they are not related to any other times. If they are contingently related to other times, they may say this as well. I'll discuss this further in a moment; but for now let this suffice for an explanation of *near* maximality. Times must also be *consistent*. To be consistent, a time must be such that possibly, every conjunct of it is true. An example of a time would be a proposition like <Obama is President and George Bush is not President and the angels are singing and two plus two is four and ... > where in the " ... " we fill in either p or not-p for every proposition p (other than propositions about the relations between times, if the time has no such relations) such that possibly every conjunct in this big conjunction is true.

The story about God's foreknowledge earlier also requires that at least some of these times can stand in temporal relations to one another. Following Crisp (2007), I characterize these temporal relations they stand in to one another are primitive,

---

[2] See Kim (1976).

[3] See, e.g., Chisholm (1979), Davidson (2003, 2004), Fine and Prior (1977), Zalta (1987), Crisp (2007), and Bourne (2006).

[4] A very similar approach is found in Bourne (2006), who says that times include only u-propositions, where propositions contain no tensed operators. Given the view developed later that tensed operators are explicable in terms of relations between times, Bourne's approach arguably implies that times do not contain propositions about their relations as conjuncts.

[5] This sort of *nearly* maximal account of times is presented as just the sort of account of times an ersatzer should prefer in Finch and Rea (2008). They don't say whether times which are in fact e-related might be contingently *fully* maximal.

unanalyzable *earlier than* relations. Saying that times can stand in such relations is unsurprising, since it is tempting to affirm that some times are indeed earlier than others and some times are later than others. Further, it is not implausible that the temporal relatedness of times explains our talk of the temporal relation of events. One event e obtains later than another event e′ just in case the time at which e′ obtains is earlier than the time at which e obtains. Saying that our times are so related, then, should not by itself sink our story as implausible.

I shall say that times which are related to one another by these earlier-than relations form a series of times. We can call such a series of times a series of *e-related* times. Such series are useful for explaining when some proposition *was* true, when some proposition *will* be true, and when some proposition *is* true in the present-tensed sense of "is" (i.e., "is currently"). This, in fact, is another valuable feature of a theory which includes times and their relations. In the world of my story, a proposition p *was* true just when that proposition is entailed by a time which is earlier than the present time. A proposition p *will be* true just when that proposition is entailed by a time which is later than the present. And, a proposition *is* true, in the present-tensed sense of "is," just when that proposition is entailed by the present time. The present time is the true time. Times, on this view, take turns being true. Indeed, propositions are true at some times and false at others. On this view, then, like others explored earlier in this text, propositions can change their truth-values.

We might ask whether all of the times are e-related to other times or whether only some are. Here again, I will follow Crisp in claiming that there is only one series of e-related times. It includes only those times that did, do, or will represent the actual world. Other times could have been e-related to one another; but as a contingent matter of fact they are not. I leave it as an exercise for the reader to explore the epistemic status of modifications of my story which do not take this answer to the question of which times are e-related.

Besides explaining what the times are, I should also say something about what God *does* with them. For, on the story sketched earlier, God *orders* the times. That is, he brings it about that they are e-related in the way that they are. I propose that he does this by willing them to be so related. He wills, for each particular time in our series, that it be earlier than some other time which be earlier than some other time, and so on.

This shouldn't be objectionable in itself. Defenders of the sort of account of times I have sketched here often take it as a primitive, unexplained matter of fact that certain times are e-related to one another rather than other times. Thomas Crisp, for instance, writes the following:

> So the suggestion here is that the *earlier than* relation connects certain abstract times and not others, though which abstract times it connects is something that could have been different. Well, one might wonder, why wasn't it different? Why does the *earlier than* relation connect just the times it does? What explains the fact that it connects these times and not others? ... [A]s plausible an answer as any to [these] questions is that it's a brute, contingent fact that the abstract times come temporally ordered as they do. Explanation has to come to an end somewhere,

and it's not unreasonable to suppose that it bottoms out in the contingent fact that certain times are earlier than certain other times. (2007: 104)

Such theorists shouldn't find it in principle objectionable, of course, if this contingent fact *does* have an explanation. Crisp, in this passage, is trying to defend the view that it is *acceptable* if the fact doesn't have an explanation—not that it is unacceptable if it does.

Furthermore, certain theists may have a special motivation for thinking that there *is* an explanation of this contingent fact, if it is a fact. For example, some theists are attracted to a strong version of the Principle of Sufficient Reason.[6] They will want an explanation for the obtaining of these temporal relations. Other theists, due to their views about divine sovereignty or creation, will not wish to have temporal relations obtaining independently of the divine will. And still others may be attracted to the idea that God can put a halt to time.[7] Any such theists should be at least somewhat attracted to the idea that God can bring it about that the times are ordered in a particular way by willing them to be so. The claim that God orders the times should not, then, by itself render my story unlikely given theism.

It is instructive to note that the story I propose allows that the very same times could have been ordered differently than they are in fact ordered. Yesterday could have been the last day of time, for example, if God had so willed it. It is in part in order to allow for this possibility that I said earlier that times are essentially only *nearly* maximal rather than maximal. For, if the times were essentially maximal and so included conjuncts about how they are related to other times, then God couldn't just relate them as he wished. He couldn't take a time t that included as a conjunct that it is earlier than a time t' and order t such that it was *not* earlier than t. For, in that case, t couldn't be true without it being the case that t was earlier than t'—which by hypothesis isn't true. In order to allow that times could have been ordered differently, I claim that times are essentially only nearly maximal rather than maximal. The times which God orders by earlier than relations to one another are the only ones which contingently say something about their relations to each other.

The features highlighted earlier are the primary metaphysical elements of the story. The primary epistemological elements of the story are what it says about God's self-awareness, his knowledge of times, and his deductive knowledge.

Part of the story is that God knows what he wills by his self awareness. This self awareness may involve introspection, or something weaker. Some may worry that introspection is a bit too strong, that it involves too much effort on God's part. Perhaps God knows what he wills, including his willing that certain times be e-related in a particular way, through some sort of self-awareness which falls short of introspection.[8] Either sort of self-awareness may plausibly lead to knowledge and even infallible

---

[6] For a defense of such a principle, see Pruss (2006).

[7] Those included will be advocates of either atemporalism (e.g., Stump and Kretzman 1981) or relative timelessness (e.g., Padgett 2012).

[8] I'm particularly attracted here to Uriah Kriegel's idea that conscious states (like God's willings) are self-representational and that we might be able to know them through their self-representation (see Kriegel (2009)).

knowledge for someone sufficiently good at using the method required. And we may suppose that God is sufficiently good here without rendering the story told earlier unlikely given theism.

The story also requires that God knows that he's omnipotent—that whatever he wills goes. Though this sort of self-knowledge on God's part is often taken for granted—it must be, for instance, an important part of the Molinist's story, too—it's not obvious how it goes. Since this is a sort of self-knowledge, we might imagine that God has it by virtue of some kind of self-awareness as in the case of his knowledge of his will. But, it is also, according to the classical theist, a metaphysically necessary fact. As such, God might know it by virtue of *a priori* reasoning. Either way, it is unlikely that the present account of God's infallible foreknowledge will be found wanting because it relies upon the claim that God has infallible knowledge of his omnipotence, as this claim is very likely given theism.

God must also know the times. But to know the times is simply to know all of the consistent combinations of propositions, excluding propositions about the relations between times. Again God may know this *a priori*. It may even be that such consistent combinations of propositions simply are ideas in God's mind. Some have defended this sort of view about possible worlds, and times on the present account parallel popular accounts of possible worlds.[9] That God has modal knowledge of this sort is, again, not unlikely given theism.

The foregoing metaphysical and epistemological elements are the only major elements necessary to make sense of the story articulated earlier. For, suppose with the elements explicated earlier that God does have infallible knowledge of his will, his omnipotence, and of the times. And suppose that God wills for these times to be ordered in a particular way. It will then follow that God has infallible knowledge that he wills the times to be ordered in the particular way that he ordains, and he has infallible knowledge that what he wills goes. If God also is infallibly competent at deduction, another element included earlier, then he can have infallible knowledge that the times *are* e-related in the particular way he has willed. And this will be plenty to ensure his infallible foreknowledge of all that occurs in the history of our world.

For, suppose that God has infallible knowledge that the times are e-related in the particular way he has willed. He will then know, for any time t, its relations to every other time. But, then, for any future truth F, God will know F. For, F will be true just in case it is entailed by a time which is later than the present time. By hypothesis, God knows infallibly the relations between the present time and every other time, including whatever time entails F. God knows infallibly, then, that F is entailed by a time that is later than the present. And this is just to say that God knows that F will be true—indeed, he even knows at which future time F will be true. And he knows this infallibly, since by virtue of his infallible deductive competence he deduces it from other things he infallibly knows.

[9]   For accounts of possible worlds which parallel the account of times presented here, see Planting (1974b), Chisholm (1976), Fine and Prior (1977), Adams (1974), and Zalta (1983). For a discussion of views according to which possible worlds and other abstracta are divine thoughts or something similar, see Morris (1987) and Menzel (1987).

So we have a story about how God might achieve infallible and exhaustive foreknowledge through time-ordering. And, so far, we have seen no reason to think that the story is one which is unlikely given theism. In the next section, I argue that the story does not require the truth of causal determinism. If the arguments of both sections are sound, then it follows that the story told earlier is an attractive conciliatory story of just the sort the incompatibilist needs to implement the strategy of Part I in response to the foreknowledge argument. For, it is a story of a not-very-low epistemic status according to which God has exhaustive and infallible foreknowledge without causal determinism being true.

2. Time-ordering and causal determinism

My argument that the story of the preceding section does not require the truth of causal determinism can be stated simply. Where "the time-ordering story" refers to the story concerning the mechanics of divine foreknowledge from the previous section, the argument runs as follows:

(1) The truth of causal determinism requires that every event be caused.
(2) The time ordering story does not require that every event be caused.
(3) So, the time-ordering story does not require the truth of causal determinism.

The intuitive idea behind the argument is simple enough. Causation is a real relation amongst things in the world which goes beyond their mere temporal relatedness. But, that God orders some times does not imply that there will be any such relations between things in the world. Nor does God's ordering times in a certain way imply that God himself causes every event. So, (2) is secure. Yet, surely the thesis of causal determinism is supposed to be about events in the world being determined by causes. If there are events in the world that are uncaused, then those events are not determined by causes. So, (1) is secure. And hence (3) follows.

While the intuitive argument is powerful as far as it goes, there is a good deal more to be said on behalf of both (1) and (2). For, against (1) it will be urged that the thesis of causal determinism is quite often defined in such a way that it does *not* require that every event be caused. And, against (2) it will be insisted that if God orders the times as in the story, then he surely does cause every event that ever occurs. I now respond to each of these concerns below.

2.1 How to define causal determinism

The first key claim in my defense of the compatibility of my story with the absence of causal determinism concerns how we understand the thesis of causal determinism. I propose that we understand causal determinism as some kind of determining by causes. Thus, I propose to define causal determinism using causation. But, as it turns out, this is frequently *not* how causal determinism has been defined. And, indeed, not only is there an alternate proposal for how to define causal determinism, which is much more commonly used in the literature on free will, but there are some common arguments urged against defining causal determinism in the way I propose. Accordingly, my approach in this section will be to rebut the common arguments against my approach to defining causal determinism and to offer an argument against the alternative approach. Against the alternative approach, I argue that someone who wishes to defend the foreknowledge argument has good reason to prefer defining causal determinism in the way I propose, and so my defining it in this way for the purpose of evaluating my story is dialectically innocent.

In what follows I will present my proposal, then present the main alternative proposal, then respond to objections to my proposal, and then present my objection to the alternative proposal. My proposal is that we define causal determinism in something like the following way:

(Causal CD) $\forall x, t$ [(x occurs at t) $\rightarrow \forall t'[(t' < t) \rightarrow (\exists y$ (y exists at t' & y is a sufficient cause of x)

In English, Causal CD says that for all events x and times t, if x occurs at t then for every time t', if t' is earlier than t, there is a y such that y exists at t' and y is a sufficient cause of x. Three things are immediately worthy of note concerning this proposal. First, it is a global proposal in that it proposes that if causal determinism is true, then *every* event is causally determined. One could of course use something much like it to define more limited notions of causal determinism. Second, it is a proposal according to which determining factors of events go all the way back to the earliest times. This feature of the proposal is important in the present context, since this is part of what enables the thesis to be useful in the free will debate. After all, if the determining factors of our actions went back only a few moments, we might wonder why this is such a threat to freedom. But, if they go back beyond our births, the worry becomes much more serious. Some authors who oppose accounts like Causal CD have opposed them on the grounds that they do not accommodate determining factors going very far back.[10] But there seems to be no problem at all with Causal CD on this score. The third feature of Causal CD also helps to explain its utility for the free will debate. It is that it requires that antecedent causes be *sufficient* causes. If it didn't require this, then one might wonder why it's truth would threaten freedom, as room would remain for us to make unique causal contributions to our actions which were not themselves explained by prior causes.

The main alternative approach to defining causal determinism is to do so using a relation of entailment rather than a causal relation. Formally, we can express the view as follows:

(Non-Causal CD) $\forall t, t', W, W', L$ ([t < t' & the world is way W' at t' & the world is way W at t and the laws of the world are L] $\rightarrow \square_L$ [(the world is way W at t & the laws of the world are L at t) $\rightarrow$ the world is way W' at t']).

---

[10] See Hoefer (2010).

In English, Non-Causal CD says that for every time t and t', way the world is W and W', and complete conjunction of laws L, if t is earlier than t' and the world is way W' at t' and way W at t and the laws of the world are L, then it is logically necessary that if the world is way W at t and the laws of the world are L, then the world is way W' at t'. Though a mouthful, the basic idea here is clear. It is logically necessary that if the world was as it in fact was and the laws are what they in fact are, then the future will be what it in fact will be. There can be no change in the way the world will be without a change in the way the world was or the laws which govern it. In a phrase, "given the way things are at a time t, the way things go thereafter is fixed as a matter of natural law" (Hoefer 2010). Since the factors which determine the way the world is according to Non-Causal CD reach just as far back as those factors which determine the way the world is according to Causal CD, and since these determining factors are logically sufficient for what they determine, at first glance it appears that Non-Causal CD is in just as good a position to guide the free will debate as Causal CD.

Despite the foregoing points of similarity between Non-Causal CD and Causal CD, philosophers who have written about causal determinism have with few exceptions[11] favored Non-Causal CD to Causal CD as capturing the thesis of causal determinism. The primary reasons for their doing so appear to be negative. That is, it appears they prefer Non-Causal CD to Causal CD because they think there are serious problems with defining causal determinism in terms of Causal CD. I'll now take up these problems one by one and argue that they are either not serious problems for Causal CD, or they are no more problems for Causal CD than for Non-Causal CD.

One kind of objection to Causal CD objects to it on the basis that it employs obscure concepts, such as causation. John Earman (1986), for example, writes that to adopt Causal CD would be to "seek to explain a vague concept—determinism—in terms of a truly obscure one—causation." A second, similar objection is that Causal CD employs concepts that do not clearly map on to anything posited by any modern physical theories. This observation is thought to tell against Causal CD because, apart from the role that causal determinism is supposed to play in the free will debate, it is also supposed to play a certain role in the assessment of physical theories. It is supposed to be the case that we can typically determine whether a physical theory implies causal determinism. Thus, if we define causal determinism in a way that employs concepts that do not clearly map on to anything in modern physical theories, the thesis cannot fulfill an important role it is supposed to have.

I don't think either of these objections is telling against Causal CD. Nor do I think either is any more telling against Causal CD than against Non-Causal CD. First, the objection based on obscurity appears to be based on the fact that there is widespread disagreement about how to understand the causal relation. There is a great variety of theories about how to understand this relation with no clear victors.[12] There are even views according to which there is no such thing as a causal relation—the causal relation makes no addition to what there is—but instead our talk of causation is made true by things other than a causal relation. But the fact that there is such disagreement does

---

[11] Mellor (1995) is one exception.
[12] For an overview, see Schaffer (2007).

not tell against Causal CD, and it does not tell uniquely against Causal CD if it does tell against Causal CD. It doesn't tell against Causal CD because there can be perfectly fine agreement amongst advocates of very different views of the causal relation about when causal predicates are appropriately applied. That is, advocates of quite diverse theories of causation may, and often do, agree about the truth-conditions for causal sentences. What they disagree about is instead what *makes* these sentences true. Thus, these theorists are likely to agree about the truth-conditions of Causal CD. And, if this is so, then it is difficult to see why Causal CD should be regarded as obscure or vague. Surely, to have explained the meaning of the thesis of causal determinism in a way that its truth-conditions will be widely agreed upon is to have gone some distance toward clarifying the thesis, rather than to have gone in the opposite direction as Earman implies. Further, even if the obscurity objection did tell against Causal CD, it would certainly tell against Non-Causal CD equally well. For, Non-Causal CD too employs language which is such that the explanation for its correct application is a matter of intense philosophical debate. It talks, for example, of times, ways the world is, and the laws. But, there is a multitude of theories about what makes applications of this language correct.[13] Even the nature of necessity is a matter of philosophical dispute, leading Mumford and Ajnum (2011: 48) to quip in Earmanian style that "to treat causation as necessity is a case of explaining a familiar notion in terms of a more obscure one"! Accordingly, the obscurity objection can hardly constitute a reason for favoring Non-Causal CD to Causal CD.

The second objection concerning the absence of clear correlates of events and causes in physical theory is somewhat better. What it shows is that if we define causal determinism using Causal CD, then in order to evaluate whether a physical theory implies causal determinism we must take on board some principles which connect the concepts of physical theory with the concepts of events and causes employed in Causal CD. If we didn't have to employ such principles, then surely the task of evaluating whether a physical theory implied causal determinism would be easier. But, a problem with this objection lurks very near. For, in order to *avoid* employing principles connecting the concepts of physical theory to those employed in a definition of causal determinism, the definition of causal determinism would have to be offered using only concepts of physical theory. But a view that uses only the concepts of physical theory is a physical thesis, not a metaphysical thesis. And causal determinism is supposed to be a metaphysical thesis! In other words, causal determinism is not supposed to be a thesis whose truth is evaluable only given the concepts of one particular physical theory. It is supposed to be a thesis which is evaluable from the perspective of a variety of different physical theories. Thus, it will not at all be surprising if it employs concepts which do not have clear correlates in modern physical theories. Further, as with the first objection presented earlier, even if this objection did cut against Causal CD, it would cut against Non-Causal CD just as well. For, many modern physical theories do not have clear correlates of times, ways the world is, or the laws any more than they have clear correlates of causes and events.[14]

---

[13] See Carrol (2010) on the metaphysics of laws and Markosian (2008) on the metaphysics of time.

[14] One very clear example is that the special theory of relativity has no place for times. See discussion in Craig and Smith (2007).

I cannot then see a reason based on these first two objections for preferring Non-Causal CD to Causal CD. The final objection sometimes raised against statements of causal determinism like Causal CD is based on the language of sufficiency employed in these statements. For, it is widely thought that causes are not sufficient in the logical sense for their effects. The same cause could have occurred and the effect not occurred, for quite a number of reasons. The game's coming on the TV can cause Ted's going to the fridge, even though the game's coming on TV does not entail that Ted goes to the fridge. Attempts to rehabilitate the notion of a sufficient cause in the face of this objection tend to involve open ended *ceteris paribus* clauses.[15] What ought to be said is that the game's coming on the TV was a sufficient cause of Ted's going to the fridge, given that no asteroid was approaching and nobody was calling with bad news, and so on and so forth. In other words, one might think that if we are to talk of sufficient causes, we might as well talk of ways the whole world is. It is really the way the world was when the game came on that is doing the work of sufficiency, if anything is, in Ted's case. Thus, we may as well abandon Causal CD in favor of Non-Causal CD, since we need *something* to do the work of sufficiency, as explained earlier.

But this objection is not persuasive either. For, there is no need to understand the sufficiency involved in sufficient causation as *logical* sufficiency. Rather, we might explicate a perfectly comprehensible notion of *causal* sufficiency. To say that x at t is a *sufficient cause* of y at t' is simply to say that either x is a cause of y and there are no other causes of y, or that x is a cause of y and x is a cause of every cause of y other than x. x, in other words, *suffices causally* for y. But this is not to say that x suffices *logically* for y. It may be possible for x to obtain and y to not obtain. But, if x obtains, then all that is required causally for y has obtained.[16] Given this alternative and attractive notion of causal sufficiency, the objection that Causal CD ultimately simply collapses into Non-Causal CD disappears. Causal CD and Non-Causal CD really are distinct views.[17, 18]

---

[15] This observation is typically traced back to (Russell 1912). As Mumford and Anjum (2011) point out, however, authors have sometimes mistakenly thought that Russell was attacking the utility of the notion of causation as applied to the sciences, when in fact he was only attacking the notion of causation *understood as necessitation* when applied to the sciences.

[16] (O'Connor and Jacobs 2013: 178) make a very similar point.

[17] It may seem at first glance as though the account of sufficient cause proposed in this paragraph would imply that worlds with causal overdetermination are worlds in which causal determinism is not true, since in those worlds there can be multiple causes of an event e where none of these causes causes the other causes of e. The difficulty can be avoided, however, if we say that in cases of genuine overdetermination, the overdetermining causes form one single causal condition which indeed does either cause the phenomenon in question by itself or else it causes every cause of the phenomenon. The overdetermining causes, taken individually, are not sufficient causes on my account. However, they could be.

[18] This explanation of sufficient cause will only be attractive if we suppose that causation is transitive. I propose that those who are inclined to deny that causation is transitive, e.g., (Hall 2000), can have the core of my proposal here if they will replace talk of sufficient causation with talk of being a member of a causal chain. Causal determinism will be the thesis that every event e at any time t' is such that for any time t earlier than t' there is something which is a member of a causal chain that contains an immediate and exclusive cause of e. Something x existing at a time t is an immediate and exclusive cause of something y just in case x causes y, and there are no other causes of y existing at t or later than t.

The objections to Causal CD can be rebutted. But, more than that, there is a serious problem with Non-Causal CD. The problem is that it cannot fulfill the role that the thesis of causal determinism is supposed to play in the foreknowledge debate. I'll start by explaining the basic idea which leads me to think that this claim is so and then offer a more careful argument in favor of it. The basic idea is as follows. In Chapter 2, we learned that the role that causal determinism should play in the foreknowledge debate is for it to be that which was required by infallible divine foreknowledge and which explains why there are no free human actions. And for causal determinism to explain why the actions of human beings are not free, casual determinism needs to say something about the explanation for human actions. But, if we define causal determinism by Non-Causal CD, then causal determinism is not a thesis involving any explanatory relations at all. And so it will not tell us anything about the explanations for human actions. It only tells us about entailment relations, and entailment relations are not explanatory relations. So, if we define causal determinism as Non-Causal CD, then causal determinism will not be able to play the dialectical role it is supposed to play in the foreknowledge debate.

Though the basic idea is powerful enough to shake our confidence in Non-Causal CD, it would be nice if this idea could be defended more carefully. Perhaps the best way to defend the idea more carefully is by considering what must be meant by a "way the world is" according to Non-Causal CD. Is it included as part of the way the world was at t_1, for example, that <Elizabeth sings a love sonnet to John at t_{100}> was true at t_1? In other words, is <Elizabeth sings a love sonnet to John at t_{100}>'s being true part of the way the world was at t_1? If so, then any world in which at all times there are truths about everything that will ever occur will be a world in which causal determinism is true, given Non-Causal CD. For, given that the way the world is at a time includes an exhaustive list of truths about the future, it follows that in such worlds the way the world is at a time all by itself entails the way the world will be. And given that entailment is monotonic, it follows that in such a world the way the world is at any time together with the laws also entails the way the world is at any later time—whether or not there *are* any laws. Further, if causal determinism is to play the role it is assigned in the foreknowledge debate, then in such a world, the thesis of causal determinism would need to explain why there are no free actions. But most philosophers are unattracted to these consequences. Few philosophers have been attracted to the idea that if an exhaustive list of propositions about the future are true in the past, then causal determinism is true.[19] And few philosophers who are attracted to the Non-Causal account of causal determinism would be attracted to the view that causal determinism could be true in a world without laws. Finally, few philosophers will be attracted to the idea that Non-Causal CD would explain why there are no free actions in such a world.

---

[19] One potential exception about which we spoke in Chapter 1 are those philosophers such as Rhoda (2007) who think that claims about the future are true only if something present *determines* them. But it is even unclear whether such philosophers would accept the view in the text, since it is not clear that they require the determining required for truth to be *causal* determining.

Suppose then that we do not include the truth of propositions about the future as part of the way the world is at a time. Is there a principled way to do so? The typical approach is to appeal to a distinction between temporally relational and temporally intrinsic features of the past. Sometimes the temporally relational features are called soft features and the intrinsic features hard features. We can then redefine Non-Causal CD using only ways the hard, or intrinsic, features of the past were.[20] The modified Non-Causal CD will say:

(Hard Non-Causal CD) $\forall$t, t', W, W', L ([t < t' & the world is way W' at t' & the hard features of the world are way W at t and the laws of the world are L] $\rightarrow \Box_L$ [(the hard features of the world are way W at t & the laws of the world are L at t) $\rightarrow$ the world is way W' at t']).

Less formally, Hard Non-Causal CD will say that, necessarily, if the past hard features of the world are as they in fact are and the laws are as they in fact are, then the future must be as it will be.

One trouble with this modification of Non-Causal CD is the same as the trouble facing the Ockhamist view of accidental necessity we discussed in Chapter 1. Namely, the advocate of this modified view faces the difficulty of clarifying the distinction between hard and soft features of the past—a task which as we saw there has proven extremely difficult. But the trouble goes even further. For, there is good reason to think that the advocate of the foreknowledge argument should not claim that Hard Non-Causal CD explains why human actions are not free.

To see why, recall that as we saw in Chapter 1, it isn't very plausible to claim that divine beliefs are not hard, intrinsic features of the past. They do not seem to be relational features of the past after all. Moreover, it is clear that the *advocate* of the foreknowledge argument should not grant that they are relational features—otherwise a premise in her argument would be false. But, these divine beliefs are also infallible. So, they are such that if God holds one about the future, this entails that the future will be as he believes it will be. But, now, just imagine a world in which God holds exhaustive beliefs about how the future will go and these beliefs are infallible. It's being the case that God holds such exhaustive beliefs and it's being the case that they are infallible will explain why causal determinism true, given Hard Non-Causal CD. For, in such a world, the way the hard features of the past are will entail the way the future is, as God's beliefs are hard features of the past and they entail the way the future is. And given that entailment is monotonic, the way the hard features of the past are together with the way the laws are will also entail the way the future is—whether there are laws or not. But, as we saw earlier, the advocate of the foreknowledge argument should claim that when causal determinism is true, it explains why there are no free human actions. Given the transitivity of explanation,[21] it will follow that the advocate of hard Non-Causal CD

---

[20] Todd (2013) discusses this account of causal determinism.
[21] More likely, the principle relied upon is one which connects truth-making with explanation, as follows: necessarily, if x makes p true and p explains q then x explains q. Cf. (Lange 2013: 256).

should claim that God's holding the beliefs he does and these beliefs being infallible explains why there are no free human actions. But, this claim is implausible, as we saw in Chapter 2. Indeed, for the advocate of the foreknowledge argument, the whole point of arguing that infallible divine foreknowledge requires causal determinism was to be able to say that something *other* than God's beliefs, and infallibility explains why human actions are not free. Embracing Hard Non-Causal CD is therefore unattractive for the advocate of the foreknowledge argument, as it requires her to make implausible claims about the explanation for why human beings lack freedom.

Causal CD is in a much better position with respect to these difficulties than is Non-Causal CD. Causal CD does not put the advocate of the foreknowledge argument in the unenvious position of needing to explicate the hard/soft distinction. And, embracing Causal CD will not require the advocate of the foreknowledge argument to embrace the claim that exhaustive divine forebeliefs together with divine infallibility explains why there are no free human actions. For, while the fact that God holds exhaustive forebeliefs about the future and is infallible makes Hard Causal CD true, it does not make Causal CD true. Thus, using Causal CD to define causal determinism should be far more attractive in the present context than we might have previously thought. Objections to defining causal determinism in terms of Causal CD are unpersuasive, and there is good reason to prefer defining causal determinism in terms of Causal CD rather than in terms of Non-Causal CD in the present dialectical context.

2.2 Whether God causes by time-ordering

Suppose, then that we define causal determinism using Causal CD. Thus, if causal determinism is true, then every event has a cause. I now want to defend my claim that the time-ordering story does not require that every event has a cause. I do so in two ways. First, I rebut the most natural arguments for the conclusion that the time-ordering story *does* require that every event has a cause. Then, I show that many incompatibilists will have significant reason to think that the time-ordering story does not imply that every event has a cause.

Some will hear my time-ordering story and think: "Surely if this story were true every event *would* have a cause. For, on the story, God orders the times, and God's ordering the times entails that every event occurs as it does. God thereby causes every event to occur as it does. So, every event has a cause—namely, God." I think this argument should be resisted.

The reason this argument should be resisted is that it relies upon some transfer principle like the following: if X causes e and <e occurs> entails <p> then X causally brings it about that p. Here causation is transferred across entailment. But, the most general such transfer principles are clearly false for causation, and it is difficult to see how some more limited such principle which applied to the case of God but not to other objectionable cases could be devised without being suspiciously *ad hoc*. The general principle just stated is clearly false in the case where p is a necessary truth, for instance. For, where p is a necessary truth, the principle would imply that anytime anyone causes anything, she also causally brings it about that this necessary truth is true, since it is entailed by every proposition. And this is surely wrong; we don't causally bring it about that necessary truths are true whenever we do anything. The principle also plausibly fails generally for contingent truths. One of the other reindeer can cause Rudolph's nose to be covered in black soot without thereby causing Rudolph to have a nose, though <Rudolph's nose is covered in black soot> entails <Rudolph has a nose>. There is, then, good reason to resist the line of argument offered earlier by my hypothetical objector who would claim that my story requires that God causes every event.

I doubt that there is any argument that my story implies that God causes every event which is as natural as the argument made earlier appealing to transfer principles governing causation. But perhaps it will be argued against my account that certain analyses of causation that philosophers have defended imply that my story implies that God causes every event. This may be so, for example, of certain versions of counterfactual accounts of causation.[22] But arguments which rely on specific analyses of causation such as this are very unlikely to persuade those incompatibilists to whom I offer my story that the story is of very low epistemic status because the theories of causation are of low epistemic status themselves. Counterfactual analyses of causation may be further unattractive to advocates of the foreknowledge argument, since such analyses may well imply that past divine beliefs about our future behaviors are under our causal control, and this fact would arguably threaten the foreknowledge argument.[23] Thus, I am pessimistic about the prospects of arguments that my story implies that God causes every event which are based on analyses of causation, too.

No further ways of arguing that my story implies that God causes every event naturally suggest themselves to the same extent as the foregoing ways. Thus, the most natural ways of arguing that my story implies that God causes every event are unpersuasive.

Are there any arguments for thinking that my story does *not* imply that God causes every event? I think so. At least, I think that there is significant reason for many incompatibilists to think my story does not imply that God causes every event. The simple argument here is that many incompatibilists are agent-causalists, but agent-causalists are likely to think there isn't anything in the story as I have described it which suggests that God causes every event.

Let me unpack the foregoing argument a bit. Agent-causalists think that when agents, such as God or human beings, cause events, it is those agents, rather than events in those agents, which cause events.[24] But, someone who advocates a view like this is unlikely to think that causation is an internal relation. That is, she is unlikely to think that, once you get the relata of the causal relation, you get the facts about how these relata are related causally.[25] When an agent A causes an effect e, it could have been that A and e existed without it's being the case that A caused e. For example, Sam may have

---

[22] See Menzies (2008) for a discussion of counterfactual theories of causation.

[23] See, e.g., Talbott (1986).

[24] See O'Connor (2000) and Lowe (2008), the latter of which was an especially significant inspiration for the way I am thinking of causation and agent-causation in this section.

[25] For more on the distinction between intrinsic and extrinsic relations, see Heil (2012).

caused Sam's arm's being raised, but it could have been that Sam and Sam's arm's being raised existed but that Sam did not cause Sam's arm being raised—imagine that instead a puppeteer who had Sam on his strings caused this. Accordingly, agent-causalists are likely to think that causation is an external relation. Facts about how relata are causally related are made true by causal relations which are real, existing entities in the world.

But now return to my story earlier. My explanation of the key metaphysical elements of that story included many things—times, temporal relations, God, propositions, etc. It even included some real causal relations. But those causal relations were only between God and earlier-than relations between times. What God was said to cause was one time's being temporally related to another. It was never said that God causes events that obtain at times—events such as Sam's raising his hand at t. But, if causal facts are made true by real causal relations as the agent-causalist will suppose, then if there are to be causal facts about God's relation to such events, God must be really causally related to those events. The only way I could see for someone to argue that my story implies that God is really causally related to events would be if she argued that times' being temporally related to one another cause the events which occur at those times. That way, my story would imply that God causes these events indirectly, by causing something that caused them. But, it is quite implausible to maintain that one time's being earlier than another causes the events which take place at those times to obtain. Thus, I find that agent-causalists will think it unlikely that my story implies that God causes every event. The second premise of my simple argument that my story does not require causal determinism, then, is defensible.

3. Conclusion

In this chapter, I began a project of contributing toward the implementation of the strategy proposed in Part I of this text for how a committed incompatibilist might use conciliatory stories to respond to the foreknowledge argument. I did so by introducing a story according to which God has exhaustive and infallible foreknowledge, arguing that the story does not require the truth of causal determinism, and arguing that the epistemic status of the story is not very unlikely given theism. If my arguments were successful, then the story qualifies as a conciliatory story of the sort discussed in Part I, and it can be disjoined with other conciliatory stories to form a formidable objection to the foreknowledge argument. In the next chapter, I seek to defend the not-unlikely status of this story given theism even further by showing that it has promising implications for theistic views of providence, and not just foreknowledge.

5

Time-ordering and Providence

This book began with two questions. First, if God knew long ago with perfection what I will do each day for the rest of my life, then how could it be that what I do each day for the rest of my life is genuinely up to *me*? Second, if much of what I will do each day for the rest of my life *is* genuinely up to me, then how could it be that *God* is in control of these things I will do? While the former is a question about the relationship between freedom and foreknowledge, the latter is a question about the relationship between freedom and providence. Through the first four chapters of this book, my focus has been rather exclusively on the question about foreknowledge. In this chapter, I turn to the question about providence.

In the previous chapter, I articulated a novel story about how God might achieve exhaustive and infallible foreknowledge through time-ordering. I argued there that the story was not of a very low epistemic status given theism and that if it were true, it wouldn't rule out human freedom by requiring causal determinism to be true. Here, by engaging with questions about divine providence, I aim to offer further support for the claim that this story is not of a very low epistemic status given theism. This is because the story contains within it an account of divine providence—an account of how God exercises control over everything that occurs in the history of the world; and, this account has features which are very attractive from the perspective of theism.

There are two features in particular on which I wish to focus. First, if providence is achieved through time-ordering in the way proposed in my story from Chapter 4, then this provides a clear avenue whereby God can exercise control over stochastic phenomena such as those we are told occur by our current physical theories. It is less clear that other accounts of the mechanics of divine providence can allow for God's control over these events. Given that a complete theory of providential control is attractive from the perspective of theism, which I shall assume here, the foregoing increases the likelihood of the present account given theism. Second, if providence is achieved through time-ordering, this provides a way to fill in the details of a concurrentist account of God's causal activity in the ordinary course of the world. Such concurrentist views have been called "eminently sane" from the perspective of theism, despite their relative unpopularity of late.[1] Further, I will show that if a concurrentist view is filled out in accordance with the time-ordering account of providence, then

---

[1] The quote is from Freddoso (1991); cf. (Freddoso 1994) on the widespread assumption of mere conservationism amongst contemporary theistic philosophers.

it will be able to escape an important objection to concurrentist views based on their apparent commitment to causal overdetermination. This, again, will help to show that given theism, the story I articulated in Chapter 4 is not very unlikely.

1. Time-ordering and stochastic phenomena

Leading physical theories are often interpreted as teaching us that there are physical events whose occurrence is not entailed by the conjunction of the laws of physics and an exhaustive conjunction of all of the facts about the state of the physical world at previous times. One commonly cited example is the decay of a radium atom.[2] The decay of a radium atom is spontaneous in exactly the sense that whether a radium atom will decay at some time is not entailed by an exhaustive conjunction of facts about the physical state of that atom and of everything else in the physical world at previous times together with the laws governing physical processes such as decay. At best, the facts and the laws determine a certain likelihood that the atom will decay.

The occurrence of such phenomena presents a problem of its own for theories of divine providence. Could even God ensure that a radium atom will decay when he wants it to? How much control does God have over such phenomena? Theists have often been attracted to the view that God at least *could* exercise complete providential control—i.e., that he can ensure that everything that occurs is subject to his will. Indeed, Kvanvig (2013) argues that there is even reason for the theist to claim that, necessarily, everything is under divine control. But one wonders exactly how God could exercise complete providence in a world with stochastic processes like the radium atom's decay.

Surely there are options a theist might pursue here. One would be simply to deny that there are or perhaps even could be genuinely stochastic phenomena. We only mistakenly think there are such because of our ignorance of the total physical facts and laws. The truth is that, given the total physical facts and laws, either the decaying or not decaying of each radium atom is indeed entailed.[3] On such a view, God could exercise complete providence simply through making use of the initial conditions and laws of the universe he designs.

Another option would be to say that in each case where a radium atom does or does not decay, God acts in a special way on the physical world to determine whether or not the atom decays. Given the total physical facts and laws by themselves, no outcome is entailed. But, God by a special act on the atoms controls their destinies. Perhaps the act is an act whereby God causes the collapses of the wave function, as in (Monton forthcoming), (Russell 2009) and (Tracy 2009). One potential advantage of this approach over the previous approach is that it would not require the violation of laws of nature.[4]

---

[2] O'Connor and Jacobs (2013) and Lowe (2013) each focus on this example. For an overview of interpretations of quantum mechanics accessible to contemporary philosophers, see Ney (2013).

[3] Famously, the Bohmian interpretation of quantum mechanics will claim this. See, e.g., Bohm and Hiley (1993).

[4] See McMullin (1993) and Murphy (2009) on the benefits of such a view.

One still further option would be an analog to the Molinist's story about providence and freedom. It is not the case that necessarily, if the physical facts are what they actually are and the laws are what they actually are, the same outcome (either decay or not decay) would obtain. However, it is nonetheless true either that were these conditions to obtain, the atom would decay or that were these conditions to obtain, the atom would not decay. God, in possession of knowledge of such a counterfactual of atom decay, could then exercise providential control over atom decay by bringing or not bringing about the antecedent of the conditional.

While each of these options is one a theist might pursue in order to defend a complete theory of providence in the face of what our current physics is often thought to teach, there are significant shortcomings of each approach. And, these shortcomings can be avoided if the theist adopts the time-ordering account of providence explained in the previous chapter.

The first option faces the shortcoming that it requires the theist to take a controversial stance on interpreting our current physical theories. As Bradley Monton (forthcoming) has recently put it, "most all physicists favor indeterministic versions" (134) of quantum mechanics. Other things being equal, a theory of complete providence which did not challenge this consensus would be better off. Furthermore, even if there *aren't* in fact stochastic phenomena in our world, there might have been. Thus, the first approach is in danger of failing to account for *necessarily* complete divine control, as Kvanvig (2013) emphasizes.

The second option requires an immense number of special and direct divine actions in the physical world. At least, such actions will be special so long as they are not the primary way whereby God exercises providence. Surely to saddle the theist with the demand that such actions are the primary way whereby God exercises providential control places quite a demand on her. A theory of complete providence that did not require these special acts would be better off, other things being equal.

Finally, the third option faces the standard problems facing Molinism more generally. It requires Exclusive Middle to hold for counterfactuals of atomic decay, and it faces a grounding objection concerning the truth of these counterfactuals. If their truth is made true by the behavior of the atoms, then it seems that their behavior is explanatorily prior to God's bringing about the circumstances in which these atoms display their behavior; but, God's bringing about these circumstances was supposed to be explanatorily prior to their behaving in the way that they do as well. And this is circular. A complete theory of providence which did not face these difficulties would again be preferable, other things being equal.

Adopting the time-ordering account of providence from the previous chapter will allow the theist a simple way to defend complete providence without facing any of the difficulties facing the three previous proposals. Suppose, for instance, that at a time t_0 a radium atom A is in a state which is such that neither its decaying nor its not decaying at a subsequent time is entailed by the total physical facts about it at t_0 together with the physical laws. Suppose, in accordance with the theory of providence presented in the previous chapter, that God orders a time t_1 later than t_0; and, according to t_1 atom A decays. Thus, by ordering t_1 later than t_0, God is able to exercise providence over whether or not A decays.

This account of God's providential control over stochastic processes has notable advantages over the alternative proposals stated earlier. First, it does not require any particular controversial interpretation of what our current physical theories teach. It can allow that these theories permit stochastic phenomena. And, even if these theories are false and there aren't in fact any stochastic phenomena, the time-ordering account of providence has the advantage of being able to sustain full providential control in possible worlds where there *are* such phenomena. Thus, it gains a notable advantage over the first alternative account of providence presented earlier.

Second, the time-ordering account does not require that when stochastic processes occur, God acts in the physical world in a special way, distinct from his general providential actions. Sure, there is divine intervention of a certain kind. But it isn't *special*; it is just the same kind of divine activity whereby God is involved in the ordinary course of nature more generally. Indeed, it may even be perfectly consistent with the laws of nature. Further, the time-ordering account gains a notable advantage over the collapse account in that it enables God to accomplish through one simple act of ordering what he must otherwise accomplish through many disparate acts of collapsing.

Finally, the time-ordering account does not face either of the difficulties faced by Molinism, as there is simply no appeal to counterfactuals here at all and so no worry about logical requirements for them or grounds for them. Other things being equal, the theist has reason to view such a proposal about divine providence quite favorably. And so, given theism, the story of the preceding chapter is again shown not to be very unlikely.

2. Time-ordering and concurrentism

As we saw in the previous section, one reason for a theist to find the time-ordering account of divine providence attractive is that it provides an account of God's providence concerning certain specific phenomena—stochastic phenomena—that has notable advantages over competing accounts of divine providence concerning those specific phenomena. But, the time-ordering account of providence is also attractive because of its account of God's non-miraculous providential control more generally. For, the time-ordering account makes available a way of filling in the details of a concurrentist view of God's non-miraculous causal involvement in the ordinary course of nature, which can help the concurrentist escape from one of the most difficult objections against her view—the overdetermination objection. Since concurrentist views allow the theist to strike an attractive balance between two more extreme approaches to God's non-miraculous causal involvement in the ordinary course of nature, the fact that the time-ordering account of providence can be used to fill in the details of a concurrentist view in this way provides one more reason to recommend it to theists.

In Section 2.1, I explain the concurrentist family of views, contrast it with its competitors, and present the overdetermination objection to concurrentist views.

In Section 2.2, I explain how the time-ordering account of providence offers the concurrentist a way to fill in the details of her view so as to escape this objection. I argue, further, that this approach to responding to the overdetermination objection has advantages over alternative approaches. Insofar as concurrentism is indeed attractive given theism, I will have provided one more reason for theists to find the time-ordering story of Chapter 4 to be of a not-very-low epistemic status.

2.1 Concurrentism and overdetermination

Some version of concurrentism has been held by a significant number of theistic philosophers since the medieval period. One finds versions of concurrentism especially among the Thomistic, Dominican, and Jesuit scholastics (e.g., Thomas Aquinas, Domingo Bañez, Luis de Molina, and Francisco Suarez)[5] as well as certain writers in the modern period (e.g., René Descartes and Gottfried Leibniz).[6] Typically, concurrentism is defined in part through its contrast with two other rival views about God's general involvement in nature.[7] These rival positions are occasionalism and mere conservationism.

The occasionalist holds that all power is God's power. According to her, no creature ever causes anything. At best, creatures might be properly *said* to cause things because God "acts in accord with a firm, though arbitrarily decreed, intention" (Freddoso1994: 133) for certain events to follow upon others. According to the occasionalist, the sunlight which beamed down on your back porch prior to the discoloring of the wood on that porch did not itself make any genuine causal contribution to this discoloration. Rather, God caused this discoloration directly and immediately all on his own, though he did so in accordance with a firm decree that sunlight should be followed by discoloration. For the occasionalist, creatures are simply the *occasions* for direct and immediate divine causation.

According to the mere conservationist, the occasionalist is doubly wrong. First, the occasionalist is wrong to relegate all power to God. Creatures, too, can make genuine causal contributions to the world. For example, a ball rolling down an incline can cause the grass beneath it to be flattened. Second, according to the mere conservationist, the occasionalist has misunderstood God's activity in the production of effects. According to the mere conservationist, God acts in the ordinary course of nature simply by "creating and conserving natural substances and their accidents, including their active and passive causal powers" (Freddoso 1994: 133). When these substances act to produce an effect, they alone are the direct and immediate cause of this effect. God is a cause of this effect only by virtue of his activity in sustaining these creatures and their

---

[5] Relevant works include: Thomas Aquinas, *Summa Theologiae* 1, q.104–5; Thomas Aquinas, *Summa Contra Gentiles* 3; (Bañez 1934), (Molina 1953), (Suarez 1965). For a contemporary discussion of these views, see Freddoso (1991 and 1994).

[6] It is more controversial whether Descartes and Leibniz are concurrentists. But, for helpful discussions indicating that they were, see Clatterbough (1995), Pessin (2003) and Whipple (2010).

[7] See, e.g., Kvanvig (2007) along with Freddoso (1991 and 1994) which I follow closely here.

powers in existence. When the grass flattens, the ball alone directly and immediately causes this; God causes it only in the attenuated sense that he conserves the ball and its powers in existence as it causes the flattening of the grass.

The concurrentist wishes to maintain a middle position between the occasionalist and the mere conservationist. With the mere conservationist and against the occasionalist, she wishes to maintain that creatures make genuine causal contributions to the world. It is perfectly correct to attribute the flattening of the grass to the ball's causal activity and not simply in the sense that the ball's rolling was the occasion of God's directly causing this flattening. However, with the occasionalist and against the mere conservationist, the concurrentist wishes to maintain that God is more immediately involved in the production of effects that are attributable to the causal activity of creatures. God causally contributes to these effects not simply by conserving those created substances which cause them but in some more immediate, intimate way. God's causal activity in bringing about the flattening of the grass is not exhausted by his conserving the ball and its powers in existence. For the concurrentist, that the grass flattens is as attributable to God as it is to the ball.

Now, it should be clear that the foregoing explanation of concurrentism leaves significant freedom for developing the specifics of a concurrentist view. For, while there are certain core commitments that concurrentists share—that creatures make genuine causal contributions to the world, that God does more than merely conserve creatures as they cause effects, that God shares responsibility with creatures for worldly effects—there are numerous ways one might imagine for a concurrentist to maintain these commitments, several of which will be explored later. For now, let the rough sketch outlined earlier suffice as a general introduction to concurrentist views.

I now turn to the concurrentist's apparent commitment to causal overdetermination, and the trouble this makes for concurrentism.[8] I'll present the argument using the example of the ball's flattening the grass by rolling, though the example generalizes to any creaturely causal activity.[9] Imagine, then, a rolling ball which I will call "B". And let the flattening of the grass which the concurrentist would wish to attribute to this ball "F". Finally, imagine that God, whom I will call "G," engages in whatever causal activity it is whereby the concurrentist will attribute F to God. We can now present the overdetermination objection to concurrentism as follows:

The Overdetermination Objection

(1) If concurrentism is true, then B causally explains F *and* G causally explains F.
(2) If B causally explains F *and* G causally explains F, then F is causally overdetermined.
(3) No events are causally overdetermined.
(4) So, concurrentism is not true.

---

[8] The objection here offered against concurrentism resembles a classic objection that Malebranche offered against the doctrine of continuous creation. For a discussion of that objection, see Miller (2011).

[9] The reader may note my preference for describing causation in terms of substances causing events by acting. For a detailed account of causation which fits this mold, see Lowe (2013).

Let us have a brief look at the premises of this argument to see why it might be thought to be a powerful objection to concurrentism.

Let us begin with premise (1). Premise (1) would seem to need little defense, as it appears to be simply a straightforward implication of concurrentism. What is distinctive about concurrentism is precisely the idea that both God and creatures are intimately causally involved in bringing about those effects which creatures causally explain. Both God and creatures are genuine causes, and the causal activity of each can be cited to explain the very same effects—in our example, effect A. But, that one can cite either G or B as an explanation for F is sufficient for each of G and B to "causally explain" F in the sense required by premise (1). So, the concurrentist is committed to premise (1). G and B each causally explains A, since each of G and B engages in causal activity and citing either offers an appropriate answer to the question, "Why did F occur?"

Much more disputable in the overdetermination objection is premise (2). Why think that the fact that each of G and B causally explains A, in the sense just articulated, implies that F is causally overdetermined? The general approach to defending (2) is as follows. When there are multiple true causal explanations for some event, that event is causally overdetermined unless one of those explanations depends upon the other in one of two ways to be articulated momentarily.[10] In other words, there are only two ways (to be explained below) in which there can be multiple true causal explanations for some phenomenon but that phenomenon *not* be overdetermined. However, as we will also see momentarily, it is difficult to see how the case of divine–creature concurrence can fit into either of these exceptional categories. Without a satisfying model for divine–creature concurrence, there is a presumption in favor of the conclusion that G's and B's causally explaining F indeed does overdetermine F.

To fill in the details of this argument in support of (2), we must attend to the two kinds of exceptional cases the argument alludes to, in which there are multiple true causal explanations of a phenomenon but that phenomenon is not thereby causally overdetermined. In each kind of case, the explanations do not overdetermine the phenomenon because at least one of the causal explanations depends on the other. First, there are cases involving *causal chains*. For example, we might explain why E occurred by saying either (1) X caused E or (2) Y caused X and X caused E. Here, each of (1) and (2) provides a causal explanation of E, but that (1) and (2) each causally explain E does not imply that E is causally overdetermined. And, this is because one of the explanations—(2)—logically depends on the other. Second, there are cases involving *causing via a part*. We might say that (1) the chair caused the depression in the carpet and (2) the chair's leg caused the depression in the carpet, in order to explain that depression. Here again, though (1) and (2) provide multiple causal explanations of the depression, that depression isn't overdetermined, since (2) arguably logically depends on (1).

Unfortunately, neither of these models is attractive from the perspective of the concurrentist. The Causation by Parts model seems wholly inappropriate

---

[10] For a helpful comparison here, consult Merricks's (2001, 2003) overdetermination argument for eliminativism.

metaphysically, as the concurrentist will not be comfortable claiming that creaturely causes such as the ball are parts of God or vice versa. And, the Causal Chains model appears to make creatures mere instruments in God's causal grasp (or vice versa).[11] Insofar as the concurrentist wishes to maintain that at least some creaturely causes, such as human beings, have some originating role to play in causation, she will not want to say that all creaturely causes are nothing but instruments of divine causation. Thus, given that these are the only models of multiple causal explanations without causal overdetermination with which we are familiar, the concurrentist is hard-pressed to deny that her view does not require causal overdetermination.

The last premise of the overdetermination objection, premise (3), claims that no events are causally overdetermined. There has been a significant amount of ink spilled on the topic of causal overdetermination in recent years.[12] One conclusion that has emerged from this literature is that there is a significant tendency on the part of contemporary philosophers to write off the possibility of causally overdetermined phenomena, or to write off theories which would require them. At the very least, it is thought that other things being equal, theories which do not require causally overdetermined phenomena are preferable to those that do. When it is shown that some theory requires causally overdetermined phenomena, this by itself is taken as a serious objection to the view in question.[13] The ultimate grounds for this move are associated with Ockham's Razor and its dictum that simpler theories are preferable to more complex ones. Thus, I will take it that, other things being equal, a concurrentist theory which did not countenance systematic causal overdetermination would be preferable to one that did.

The overdetermination argument is valid. And, we have now seen a defense of its key premises. In the next section, I discuss the prospects for a concurrentist response, and argue that an attractive response can be given if the concurrentist will adopt the time-ordering account of providence.

2.2 Time-ordering and overdetermination

Given that premise (1) of the overdetermination objection is true by definition of concurrentism and that denying premise (3) would be a last resort, it appears that the best place for a concurrentist to look for a response will be to challenge premise (2). We saw earlier that the defense of premise (2) rested on the fact that the most familiar models of multiple legitimate causal explanations of a phenomenon which do not require causal overdetermination do not fit well with concurrentism. But, the concurrentist might suggest that there are, in addition to those models, other less familiar models

---

[11] This is not to say that the model has had no supporters. Aquinas, for example, is fond of explaining God's concurrence using the analogy of a person causing something by using an instrument. See, e.g., *Summa Contra Gentiles* 3. For a discussion of the potential threat here to human freedom, see Dvořák (2013).

[12] See, e.g., the debate between Merricks (2001), Sider (2003), and Merricks (2003) and the overview in Korman (2011).

[13] One excellent example here is Kim's (2005) influential exclusion argument.

which do fit better with her theory. Here, I can think of three general approaches, one of which is well suited to be employed by the advocate of the time-ordering account of providence. I will start by presenting each of these models generally and explaining which model can be adopted by the advocate of time-ordering. I then argue that this latter model has certain notable advantages over the others, though I will not argue that these advantages provide compelling reason to accept it over the other models.

First, consider the Joint Causation model.[14] According to this approach, B and G each causally explains F, though B and G are not independent causal explanations of F. They depend on each other because, taken independently, they are explanatorily inadequate for G. A classic example of such a case is where you and I together push my stalled car into my garage. I engage in some causal activity whereby the car's being in the garage is attributable to me, and you do the same. But there is no causal overdetermination here because each of us depends on the other to get the car moved. On our own, we couldn't have done it. The same applies to the case of God and the ball. God and the ball jointly cause the flattening of the grass, but this does not require overdetermination because God and the ball depend on each other in bringing about this effect.

Second, take the Causal Pluralist model. Causal Pluralism is the view that there are multiple irreducibly fundamental causal relations.[15] For instance, some have argued that there is one kind of causation—mental causation—and another very different kind of causation—physical causation. Someone who embraced this sort of Causal Pluralist view might claim that a single physical event E has a mental cause M and a physical cause P and that M's causing E depends on P's causing E. Presumably, the dependence here would involve some kind of asymmetric metaphysical relation between the mental and the physical, such as supervenience or realization.[16] One might imagine a concurrentist appealing to such causal pluralism in order to model divine–creature concurrence. For example, in order to apply this model to the grass-flattening case, the concurrentist Causal Pluralist might argue that God *divinely* causes F, that the ball *creaturely* cause F, and that God's divinely causing F depends upon the ball's creaturely causing F and/or vice versa. It seems to me that some of the medieval Christian Aristotelians may have had this sort of Causal Pluralist view in mind. When they talk of God causing the "universal *esse*" of effects and of creatures causing the "specific form" of this *esse*, I am tempted to understand them as claiming something like that God *universal-esse*-wise causes these effects and creatures *specific-form-esse*-wise cause these effects. The distinction seems to be like that between material and formal causes, where the latter is clearly a case of causal pluralism.[17]

A third and final way to model multiple dependent causal explanations in such a way that divine–creature concurrence might fit the model is as follows. Suppose a cause, C2, causes an effect, E. Now, there are some relations which obtain between C2

---

[14] Fredosso (1994) appears friendly toward this view.
[15] For a recent defense, see Jaworski (2011).
[16] For a variety of ways to explain such relations, see Fine (2001) and Audi (2012).
[17] For more quotes from medieval thinkers to this effect, see Freddoso (1991 and 1994).

and E. Chiefly, there is the causal relation between C2 and E. And, there may also be other relations which are required for this causal relation to hold. Now, imagine that we claim that a second cause, C1, causally explains why these relations between C2 and E hold. To use a diagram, we would have:

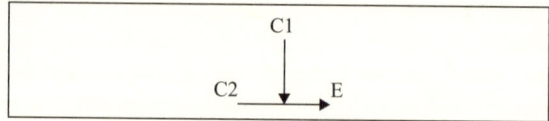

In such a case, it is plausible that we could have multiple causal explanations of E which would not require overdetermination because of their dependence on one another. C2's occurring is a causal explanation of E. And, C1's occurring is a causal explanation of E. But, these causal explanations of E are not independent. For, the latter entails the former. So, we have multiple causal explanations of E and these explanations are dependent upon one another, since one entails the other.

Recently, Ned Markosian (2012) has proposed an account like this that he thinks compatibilists about free will might be able to use in order to reconcile their views with the existence of agent causation. On Markosian's model, cause C2 in our diagram would be a human agent, and cause C1 would be some past event—like C2's having a certain property. C1 (the event in the agent) would cause not the agent but the agent's causing of the event E. The idea, then, that there might be causes of those relations which obtain between causes and effects is not without its contemporary defenders.

What is relevant for our discussion here is that the concurrentist might attempt to model divine–creature concurrence in this sort of way. She would suggest that creatures causally explain effects—that, say, that B causally explains A. And, she would then say that God causally explains some relations between B and A. Of course, it is precisely at this juncture where appealing to the time-ordering story can be helpful. For, it can help to explain exactly how God can cause relations to obtain between a creature and the effect which is attributable to it. For example, God causes B—the rolling ball—to be earlier than F—the flattened grass—by ordering the time at which B is rolling earlier than the time at which F obtains. Further, if this is how God causes relations to obtain between creaturely causes and their effects, then it is plausible that God's causal activity will depend in a variety of ways on creaturely causal activity, thereby eliminating the concern about causal overdetermination. For example, G's causally explaining F, since this is accomplished by ordering the rolling ball, B, earlier than F, will *entail* B's causally explaining F. And, it may even be that God orders the times in the way that he does in part because of what occurs at these times. Thus, for instance, he might order the time at which F occurs later than the time at which B is rolling in part *because* B is rolling at that time. But, if this is the case, then we have another way in which divine causal activity depends on creaturely causal activity. Thus, there is good reason to think that the time-ordering model can be used by the concurrentist to defend the appropriate attribution of both divine and creaturely causal explanations without requiring causal overdeterminism, because the divine and creaturely causal explanations are not independent.

Now, I do not think there are compelling reasons to favor the time-ordering approach to defending concurrentism to the Joint Causation approach or the causal pluralism approach. However, I will close this section by arguing that there are at least certain non-negligible advantages that the time-ordering approach has over these other approaches.

Take first the Joint Causation approach. This approach arguably should not satisfy the concurrentist.[18] For, the concurrentist wishes to maintain that both creatures and God are genuine causal explainers. Both engage in causal activity which explains the effect in question. For example, the one effect F is supposed to be causally explained both by G and by B. But, the Joint Causation model appears not to allow this. Rather than allowing that there are at least two causal explanations of F, the aforementioned response appears to allow only one, joint, causal explanation—*B and G together*. Analogously, in the car pushing case, there is one causal explanation of the car's movement—*the joint activity of me and you together*—and not two causal explanations—my pushing activity on the one hand and yours on the other. Surely, there would be something inappropriate in attributing the car's being in the garage to either you or me individually; it's being there is attributable only to *both* of us. But, this is not what the concurrentist wants to say about divine and creaturely causal activity. On the other hand, according to the time-ordering approach it really is appropriate to attribute the effect, F, to each of G and B. At least, it is certainly not clear that such attributions are *inappropriate*, as it is on the Joint Causation approach.

Take, second, the Causal Pluralist approach. One significant difficulty with this approach is that it simply isn't clear how it escapes causal overdetermination in the concurrentist case. Sure, there are different *kinds* of causes of F—divine and creaturely causes. But, why should that suggest that the effect isn't causally overdetermined? In other cases, such as the mental-physical case, the pluralist avoids overdetermination by claiming that the causes are not independent because some kind of metaphysical relation of explanation obtains between the physical causes and the mental causes. But, the asymmetric metaphysical dependence relations typically appealed to here will not be relations the concurrentist will want to say apply in the creaturely-divine case. Neither the divine causal explanation nor the creaturely causal explanation supervenes on or realizes the other. So, it is difficult to see how divine causal explanation of effects depends on creaturely causal explanation (or vice versa) on this approach in such a way as to pacify the concern about overdetermination.

This same worry does not crop up for the time-ordering account. For, the advocate of this account has promising ways of explaining the dependence of divine causal explanation on creaturely causal explanation. There is arguably both dependence in the form of entailment (i.e., logical dependence) as well as dependence in the form

[18] For two recent authors who have argued against this Joint Causation model for divine concurrence, see Miller (2011) and Mancha (2001).

of explanation (explanatory dependence). Thus, the time-ordering approach will be less vulnerable to the charge of overdetermination than the causal pluralism approach.

Let me summarize. We have seen in this section that the time-ordering account of providence from the previous chapter arguably provides the concurrentist with a way to respond to a very important objection to her view. Insofar as concurrentism is an attractive position from the perspective of theism, this bodes well for the time-ordering account. Further, there is at least some reason to think that the time-ordering approach to defending concurrentism is preferable to other approaches to defending concurrentism. Thus, all the more, what we are seeing is that the time-ordering story does not have a very low epistemic status given theism.

3. Conclusion

In this chapter, I continued my defense of the not-very-low epistemic status given theism of the time-ordering account of the mechanics of divine foreknowledge and providence articulated in Chapter 4. We saw here that the time-ordering story offers attractive benefits to the theist concerning divine governance of stochastic phenomena in particular and concerning God's non-miraculous, general causal involvement in the ordinary course of nature as well. While I will not claim that the time-ordering story has a high epistemic status for the theist, what we are seeing is that there is more and more reason to think that its status is significant enough to make a valuable contribution to a response to the foreknowledge argument which employs conciliatory stories in the manner discussed in Part I of this text.

6

The Value and Future of the Time-ordering Story

In the previous four chapters of this book, I developed and implemented a strategic response to the foreknowledge argument presented in Chapter 1. The response did not involve denying any particular premise or inference in the foreknowledge argument. Rather, it first involved showing that we are in a position to know that the foreknowledge argument is sound only if we are in a position to know that infallible divine foreknowledge requires the truth of causal determinism; and, second, it involved showing that we are not in a position to know that infallible divine foreknowledge requires the truth of causal determinism. The general strategy I proposed for arguing that we are not in a position to know that infallible divine foreknowledge requires the truth of causal determinism involves telling conciliatory stories of varying epistemic status according to which God has infallible and exhaustive foreknowledge but causal determinism is not true. In the previous two chapters, I implemented this strategy by telling a conciliatory story according to which God achieves infallible and exhaustive foreknowledge via time-ordering and by arguing that this conciliatory story is not of a very low epistemic status given theism. In this concluding chapter, I want to assess the value and future of this proposed response to the foreknowledge argument—both the general conciliatory story strategy and the time-ordering implementation of that strategy.

Assessing the value and future of this response requires us to attend to two kinds of question. The first kind of question concerns the sufficiency of the present response. Here, we must ask the following. Is the response developed here a successful response to the foreknowledge argument? Is the response sufficient to show that we are not in a position to know that the foreknowledge argument is sound? If not, what further work is needed for the response to do this? The second kind of question concerns the necessity of the present response. Here we must ask whether there are not other, perhaps simpler, ways of showing that we are not in a position to know that the foreknowledge argument is sound—ways which do not involve telling conciliatory stories at all.

This chapter addresses these questions in three parts. First, in Section 1, I return to the criteria for successful responses to the foreknowledge argument laid out in Chapters 1 and 2. I argue that the present response meets these criteria. This is no trivial feat, since arguably none of the responses to the foreknowledge argument we discussed in Chapter 1 were able to satisfy these criteria. Nonetheless, it does not by itself imply that the response is successful, as these conditions were merely necessary conditions for a successful response to the foreknowledge argument. In order for us to determine whether the present response is successful, we must attend to the question of whether the present response in fact shows that we are not in a position to know that the foreknowledge argument is sound. In the second section, I consider whether there isn't a much simpler way to show that we are not in a position to know that the foreknowledge argument is sound. I explain why recent attempts to show that there is a way to do this fail. This only further motivates us to consider the question of to what extent the present response shows that we are not in a position to know that the foreknowledge argument is sound. So, I turn in Section 3 to consider this topic. In particular, I address three significant concerns which would challenge the epistemic status of the time-ordering story. I propose ways that an advocate of the time-ordering story might address these concerns and point toward promising avenues for future development of the story.

1. Time-ordering and the success conditions

In this section, I argue that the response to the foreknowledge argument developed in the previous four chapters satisfies the three criteria for a successful response to the foreknowledge argument articulated in Chapters 1 and 2. On its own, this does not imply that the response is successful, as these conditions were merely necessary conditions for a successful response to the foreknowledge argument. Nonetheless, it is no mean feat as arguably no response to the foreknowledge argument discussed in Chapter 1 satisfied these criteria.

The three criteria for a successful response to the foreknowledge argument articulated in Chapters 1 and 2 were as follows:

(1) First, a successful response must not merely identify a technical flaw in the foreknowledge argument thereby leaving open the success of an only slightly modified version of that argument.
(2) Second, a successful response must accommodate the widely shared idea that the foreknowledge argument has more going for it than the argument for logical fatalism.
(3) Third, a successful response must not threaten the argument for causal fatalism, or the basic idea behind it, as much as it threatens the foreknowledge argument.

I'll argue that each of these criteria is satisfied by the conciliatory story response to the foreknowledge argument developed in the previous four chapters.

First, the conciliatory story response does not merely identify a technical flaw in the foreknowledge argument, thereby leaving open the success of an only slightly modified version of that argument. Indeed, the conciliatory story response does not even engage the technical details of the foreknowledge argument. Rather, the approach of the conciliatory story response has two parts, neither of which depends in any way for its success on the details of a presentation of the foreknowledge argument. The first step is to argue that we are in a position to know that the foreknowledge argument is sound only if we are in a position to know that infallible divine foreknowledge requires the truth of causal determinism. The second step argues that we are not in a position to know that infallible divine foreknowledge requires the truth of causal determinism. Importantly, the argument in defense of the first step of this strategy—the only step which refers to the foreknowledge argument—does not involve essential reference to any of the details of a statement of the foreknowledge argument. The defense of that step simply involves showing that if the existence of infallible divine foreknowledge implies that human beings lack freedom, then infallible divine foreknowledge must require something which makes human beings lack freedom and that the best candidate for this something is the truth of causal determinism. Defending these claims does not involve rejecting a premise in the foreknowledge argument on the basis of a technical flaw.

Of course, the advocate of the foreknowledge argument might challenge the steps of this strategy. I will consider some ways in which she might do so in Section 3. But, challenging the steps of the strategy in this way will not show that the strategy itself involves rejecting a premise in the foreknowledge argument on the basis of a technicality. Thus, the conciliatory story response satisfies condition (1).

It also satisfies condition (2). For it can accommodate the widely shared intuition that the foreknowledge argument has more going for it than does the argument for logical fatalism. To see this, notice that the advocate of the conciliatory story response thinks that the plausibility of the foreknowledge argument depends upon the plausibility of the idea that infallible divine foreknowledge requires something which makes human beings lack freedom. Presumably, she will also think that the plausibility of the argument for logical fatalism depends upon the plausibility of the idea that the past truth of propositions about the future requires something which makes human beings lack freedom. But, it is far more plausible that infallible divine foreknowledge requires something that makes human beings lack freedom than it is that the past truth of propositions about the future requires something that makes human beings lack freedom. For, there is a very powerful argument that infallible divine foreknowledge requires the truth of causal determinism—an argument I presented in Chapter 2. On the other hand, while the view that the past truth of propositions about the future requires the truth of causal determinism is not unheard of, it is certainly a minority position. Since most of those philosophers who regard the foreknowledge argument as better off than the argument for logical fatalism think that human freedom is incompatible with causal determinism, it follows that the advocate of the conciliatory story response can accommodate the prevalence of the intuition that the foreknowledge argument is better off than the argument for logical fatalism. That intuition is prevalent, she can say, because incompatibilism is prevalent, and because it is more plausible that infallible divine foreknowledge requires causal determinism than that the past truth of propositions about the future requires causal determinism.

Let us turn finally to success criterion (3)—that a successful response to the foreknowledge argument must not equally threaten the idea behind the argument for causal fatalism. It is again clear that the conciliatory story strategy satisfies this criterion. For, it is a key claim of the conciliatory story strategy that the best candidate for that which is both required by infallible divine foreknowledge and which explains why human beings lack freedom is the truth of causal determinism. And this claim is defended, in part, on the basis of the idea that *if* causal determinism were true, it is plausible that it would explain why there are no free human actions. Thus, the advocate of the conciliatory story strategy makes it part of her response to the foreknowledge argument that the idea behind the argument for causal fatalism is plausible.

The conciliatory story strategy, then, satisfies all three of the criteria articulated in Chapters 1 and 2 for a successful response to the foreknowledge argument. Since, as I argued in Chapter 1, it is plausible that many other responses to the foreknowledge argument do not satisfy these criteria, it follows that the conciliatory story strategy has a value that many other responses to the foreknowledge argument arguably do not have. There are, however, some strategies of responding to the foreknowledge argument that were not represented in Chapter 1. And this is because, like the conciliatory story strategy, they do not involve denying a premise of that argument. Some of these strategies are quite simple too—much simpler than the conciliatory story strategy. Thus, to continue assessing the value of the conciliatory story strategy, we must consider whether one of these simpler alternative strategies might challenge the foreknowledge argument just as well as the conciliatory story strategy. If so, then the value of the conciliatory story strategy is not so special; but if not, the value of the conciliatory story strategy is all the more special.

2. Alternative, simpler strategies

There are two strategies I know of in the recent literature on freedom and foreknowledge which challenge foreknowledge arguments without arguing that any particular premise of these arguments is false. I argue here that these strategies are quite unpersuasive.

The first strategy owes to Ted Warfield (1997, 2000). Warfield offers what he calls an "offensive strategy" on behalf of the compatibilist about freedom and foreknowledge, which involves making a positive case for the compatibility of freedom and foreknowledge, rather than making a negative case against arguments for their incompatibility. As it turns out, Warfield's argument for the compatibility of freedom and foreknowledge is quite simple. The argument is represented below, where P = Elizabeth freely sings a love sonnet to John at t_{100}, Q = It was true at t_1 that Elizabeth sings a love sonnet to John at t_{100}, and K = God knows at t_1 that Elizabeth sings a love sonnet to John at t_{100}. Assuming that Q is in fact true, we can represent Warfield's argument as follows:

(1) $\Diamond_L (P \& Q)$
(2) $\Box_L (Q \leftrightarrow K)$
(3) $\Diamond_L (P \& K)$ [from (1)–(2) and classical logic]

Given that Elizabeth's signing at t_{100} was selected arbitrarily, it follows that if the argument is sound, then it shows that infallible and exhaustive divine foreknowledge is compatible with human freedom.

It is perhaps best to interpret Warfield's argument as aimed toward classical theists who believe that necessarily, at all times, God knows all true propositions. Such theists will accept (2). Warfield is clear that he does not intend to argue for (2). Thus, it is reasonable to think of his argument as aimed toward showing that *if* (2) is true, then it is possible for God to foreknow the free actions of creatures. Unfortunately, there is a problem with premise (1) of the argument—a problem identified clearly by Peter Graham (2008). The problem is that premise (1) is question-begging in this particular dialectical context, where (2) is assumed. In defense of (1), Warfield appeals to common philosophical consensus according to which the argument for logical fatalism is not sound. But, this consensus was reached by philosophers who were not assuming (2). Graham summarizes the difficulty thus: "As support for [premise (1), Warfield] points to the fact that nearly every participant to the debate accepts the falsity of logical fatalism. Appealing to this consensus, however, renders the argument question-begging for that consensus has emerged only against the backdrop of an assumption that there is no necessarily existent omniscient being" (75). Another way to state the problem is as follows. Claim (2) commits its proponent to the view that the past truth of <Elizabeth sings a love sonnet to John at t_{100}> requires God's infallibly foreknowing <Elizabeth sings a love sonnet to John at t_{100}>. Thus, proponents of (2) should only think that (1) is true—i.e., that the past truth of <Elizabeth sings a love sonnet to John at t_{100}> is compatible with Elizabeth's *freely* singing—if they think that (3) is true—that God's infallibly foreknowing that Elizabeth will sing is compatible with her singing freely. Premise (1) therefore assumes the point to be proved.

This is not to say that nothing interesting is to be learned from Warfield's argument. What is to be learned, and what arguably has not sufficiently been learned, is that the classical theist who accepts (2) should not be so quick to agree with the common consensus that the past truth of propositions about what human beings will do is compatible with human freedom. The point may be put perspicuously by employing language I have introduced here concerning the conciliatory story strategy. The classical theist who accepts (2) has additional reason to think that the past truth of propositions about what human beings will do requires something which makes human beings lack freedom. She has this additional reason because she believes that the past truth of these propositions requires that God has infallible foreknowledge concerning what human beings will do, and because there are powerful reasons for thinking that infallible divine foreknowledge requires something that makes human beings lack freedom. Thus, Warfield's argument teaches us an important lesson, but it remains quite unpersuasive as a response to foreknowledge arguments.

A second simple response to foreknowledge arguments which does not require denying any particular premise in those arguments has recently been advocated by several writers[1] but has been defended at greatest length and in most detail by Trenton

---

[1]   In addition to Merricks's works discussed in the text, see McCall (2011) and Westphal (2011).

Merricks (2009, 2011a). The version of the foreknowledge argument that Merricks attacks is much simpler than the one laid out in Chapter 1 here. It runs as follows, where Jones and his act of sitting at t, where t is later than a thousand years ago, are selected arbitrarily:

(1) Jones has no choice about God's believing a thousand years ago that Jones sits at t.
(2) Necessarily, if God believed that Jones sits at t a thousand years ago, then Jones sits at t.
(3) So, Jones has no choice about Jones's sitting at t.

Merricks objects that the argument begs the question at premise (1). He provides a simple argument in favor of this judgment.

Merricks's argument that (1) presupposes (3), as I understand it, has two premises. The first is:

> (4) For all S and all God's beliefs b, that S has no choice about whether God has belief b presupposes (in the sense of "presupposes" relevant to begging the question) that S has no choice about what God's having belief b depends on. (2009: 53)

Merricks defends this claim on the basis of considering how we would respond to a parody of the argument from (1)–(3). In the parody, we replace Jones's sitting at t with your eating lunch at noon tomorrow, and we replace God's believing a thousand years ago that Jones will sit at t with God's believing at noon tomorrow (or at a later time) that you eat lunch at noon tomorrow. Merricks suggests that all parties to the foreknowledge debate, even those who grant that foreknowledge is incompatible with freedom, should claim that the resulting parody argument is not a good argument. And, the best way to explain why it is not a good argument is to claim that its first premise—the claim that you do not have a choice about God's belief that you eat lunch at noon tomorrow—presupposes its conclusion, namely, that you do not have a choice about your eating lunch tomorrow. That we should claim that the premise of the parody argument presupposes its conclusion shows us that (4) is true—i.e., that a claim that one does not have a choice about some of God's beliefs presupposes that one does not have a choice about that on which those beliefs depend.

The second premise in Merricks's argument that (1) presupposes (3) is:

> (5) God's belief a thousand years ago that Jones will sit at t depends upon Jones's sitting at t.

From (4) and (5) it follows that (1) presupposes (3) in the sense relevant to begging the question. However, in favor of (5), Merricks writes only the following:

> My objection to [the argument from (1)–(3)] builds on an idea that goes back at least to Origen, who says: " ... it will not be because God knows that an event will occur that it happens; but, because something is going to take place that it

is known by God before it happens." Similarly, I say that God has certain beliefs about the world because of how the world is, was, or will be—and not vice versa. For example, God believes *that there are no white ravens* because there are no white ravens, and not the other way around. And God believed, a thousand years ago, *that Jones sits at t* because Jones will sit at t, and not the other way around. (52)

I shall argue that in virtue of offering this and only this defense of (5), Merricks's response to foreknowledge arguments is deeply unpersuasive. There are three ways one might interpret the above passage. But none will supply an adequate defense of the claim that God's belief a thousand years ago that Jones will sit at t depends on Jones's sitting at t.

On the first reading of the passage, Merricks is simply voicing his agreement with Origen. The passage should be read as follows: "Origen says p. And so do I." If we take the passage in this way, and it is not clear that we should not, then Merricks is not *intending* to offer a defense of the claim that God's belief a thousand years ago that Jones will sit at t depends on Jones's sitting at t. He is just saying that he (and Origen) thinks this is true. Of course, that is not an adequate defense of claim (5).

On the second reading, Merricks is offering an argument from authority. "Origen says p. So, p." But while this interpretation will provide a defense of the claim that God's belief a thousand years ago that Jones will sit at t depends on Jones's sitting at t, it will not provide an *adequate* defense. The same kind of argument from authority could be championed by advocates of any number of responses to the foreknowledge argument, and the defender of the foreknowledge argument will hardly be impressed.

The final interpretation is to take Merricks as offering a defense of (5) in the form of a disjunctive syllogism, as follows:

(6) Either God's belief a thousand years ago that Jones will sit at t depends on Jones's sitting at t or Jones's sitting at t depends on God's belief a thousand years ago that Jones will sit at t.

(7) It is not the case that Jones's sitting at t depends on God's belief a thousand years ago that Jones will sit at t.

(8) So, God's belief a thousand years ago that Jones will sit at t depends on Jones's sitting at t.

Here, we get a defense of the central claim in need of defense. And it is an argumentative defense that is more than an argument from authority. Unfortunately, it commits the fallacy of a false dilemma. For, there are other options besides God's belief a thousand years ago depending on Jones's sitting at t and Jones's sitting at t depending on God's belief a thousand years ago that Jones will sit; and some of these options have figured saliently into historical and contemporary discussions of the foreknowledge argument. In particular, there is the option according to which *both* God's belief a thousand years ago that Jones will sit at t *and* Jones's sitting at t depend on *something about the world a thousand years ago* (other than God's belief itself).

What could it be about the world a thousand years ago upon which both God's belief a thousand years ago and Jones's sitting at t could depend? Perhaps the best candidate here is total facts about the spatiotemporal world a thousand years ago together with the laws governing that world. Or perhaps it is, to borrow a phrase from Merricks (2011b) himself, the world's "subjunctive aspect" a thousand years ago of being such that were Jones to encounter the circumstances which will in fact precede his sitting, he would sit together with God's determination a thousand years ago to bring those circumstances about. Or perhaps it is something else still. Regardless of what exactly it might be, this entire category of options has been overlooked in Merricks's discussion. That is quite a false dilemma indeed! So, what Merricks says in defense of a central claim in his objection to foreknowledge arguments is unpersuasive.

In this section, we saw that two recent attempts to offer a simple response to a foreknowledge argument which does not involve denying a premise in that argument are each unpersuasive. This serves to reaffirm the unique value of the conciliatory story strategy and the time-ordering implementation of that strategy, if these are indeed successful. I turn my attention to the question of whether and to what extent they are in the final section.

3. Objections, responses, and future opportunities for the time-ordering story

In Section 1, we saw that the conciliatory story strategy satisfies certain criteria for a successful response to the foreknowledge argument that are arguably not satisfied by responses to that argument that reject one of its premises. Then, in Section 2, we saw that other responses to the foreknowledge argument which do not involve denying a particular premise of that argument are not well-supported. These considerations should motivate significant interest in carefully evaluating just how successful the conciliatory story strategy is.

The success of the conciliatory story strategy depends crucially on the ability of its advocates to offer conciliatory stories of not very low epistemic status given theism, according to which God achieves exhaustive and infallible foreknowledge without causal determinism being true. The more such stories, and the higher their epistemic status, the more successful is the strategy. Aside from clearly articulating exactly how the conciliatory story strategy is itself supposed to work as a response to the foreknowledge argument, my primary contribution to this strategy in this text has been to articulate and defend one novel conciliatory story: the time-ordering story. My evaluation of the success of the conciliatory story strategy here will therefore focus on the epistemic status of this story. But, the reader is cautioned that she should not conclude that the conciliatory story strategy itself is unsuccessful if she thinks, contrary to what I claim here, that the time-ordering story is of an extremely low epistemic status given theism.

Because I have already offered some positive considerations in favor of the not-very-low epistemic status of the time-ordering story, I here want to focus on objections to that story I have commonly heard which threaten to show that it after all does have an extremely low epistemic status given theism. These objections are of three kinds. The first objects to the metaphysics of time required by the story on the basis that it is simply a bad metaphysics of time. The second objects that the metaphysics of time required by the story is inconsistent with human freedom. And, the third objects that the story is unmotivated from the perspective of theism, since even if it permits human freedom, it permits it in a way that is not useful for helping to provide a response to the problem of evil. I will offer modest responses to each of these kinds of objection here. My modest responses will often have implications for the future of the time-ordering strategy in that those who find the strategy attractive will in the future want to be able to say more to develop these responses.

3.1 Time-ordering and time

Objections to the time-ordering story which claim that its metaphysics of time is just a bad metaphysics of time may be divided into three kinds. There are objections to the claim that there are times, objections to the claim that the intrinsic nature of times is the way the time-ordering story says it is, and objections to the claim that times with the nature of those in the time-ordering story can be ordered in the way the story says they can be.

Objections to the claim that there are times of which I am aware are either objections based on metaphysical considerations or objections based on scientific considerations. The objections based on metaphysical considerations might be positive in that they attempt to show that the supposition that there are times leads to contradiction or conflicts with other independently plausible metaphysical theses. Alternatively, they might be negative in that they attempt to show that there is a rival account of the phenomena for which the existence of times is supposed to account where the rival account of these phenomena is theoretically preferable to any account of them which appeals to the existence of times. An example of a positive argument against the claim that there are times is McTaggert's (1993) argument for the unreality of time. Understood as an argument that there are no times, McTaggert should be understood as claiming that, first, if there were times, they would have to have the properties of pastness, presentness, and futurity (i.e., the A-properties) and that, second, nothing could have these properties as they are incompatible. An example of a negative argument would be the Aristotelian argument that claims which seem to be about times are in fact explicable as being made true by (temporal) relations between substances, rather than by times. The primary objection to the view that there are times based upon scientific considerations is the objection that the claim that there are times conflicts with the special theory of relativity as explained in (Minkowski 1952), where this theory is taken to imply that there is no absolute simultaneity but only simultaneity relative to a reference frame.

I do not think that these objections (and others like them) by themselves or taken together show that the time-ordering story has an extremely low epistemic status. This is because, quite independently of any concern for defending the time-ordering strategy, there are significant obstacles facing these arguments. This is hardly the place for me to enter into a deep and careful analysis of these arguments. And, I doubt that I have anything to say about them apart from what others have already said. But, briefly, I note that McTaggert's argument would seem to prove too much—not just that there are no times but that nothing is temporally related, and insofar as change requires temporal relations there is no change. The Aristotelian argument seems to leave certain explicable facts unexplained—e.g., that certain substances are simultaneous with one another is contingent, but appears to be unexplained. This fact could of course be explained quite well if we adopted times. And, finally, there are empirically equivalent versions of the special theory of relativity which do allow for absolute simultaneity, as is made clear in (Craig and Smith 2007). These brief remarks, of course, do not show that the objections above have no force against the time-ordering strategy. And, it would be desirable in the future for advocates of the time-ordering strategy to develop further responses to these objections and arguments in favor of the view that there are times. I think they are, however, enough to show that the prospects of defending the not very low epistemic status of the time-ordering story are good enough to warrant a continued pursuit.

In addition to objections to the view that there are times, there are also objections to the view that times have the intrinsic nature the time-ordering story says they do—namely, that they are nearly maximal consistent conjunctions of propositions. Again, the objections may be positive in that they directly attack this characterization of the intrinsic nature of times or they may be negative in that they argue that an alternative conception of times, say as concrete slices of reality, is preferable. In response, it is noteworthy that the account of times appealed to in the time-ordering story has had an impressive range of defenders. This is presumably because it promises to explain a wide range of data. For example, philosophers such as Thomas Crisp (2007) who are attracted to presentism have thought that a view of times such as that presented here is the best way to defend their view against the most powerful objections which threaten it. The advocate of the time-ordering story might, then, look to these resources to defend the view about the intrinsic nature of times which figures into her story. A different and perhaps more interesting response to these objections is also worth pursuing. It is to attempt to show that a concretist account of the intrinsic nature of times will produce a conciliatory story with the same relevant features—e.g., infallible foreknowledge without causal determinism—as is allowed by the abstract view of times relied upon in this text. I myself see no immediate obstacle to developing such a story. So, again, I am not persuaded that the present objections show that the defense of the not very low epistemic status of the time-ordering story (or a story much like it) is in jeopardy. Rather, they provoke future work defending the abstract account of times employed in the text as well as future inquiry into whether a story much like that defended here might be developed employing an alternative account of the intrinsic nature of times.

The final kind of objection to the metaphysics of time employed in the time-ordering story objects to the idea that times, even the abstract times of the time-ordering story, can be ordered. The best reason I can think of for why someone would hold that times cannot be ordered is that she thinks that their relations to one another are necessary. But, if someone accepts the account of times explained in Chapter 4, then for her to claim that these times are necessarily related as they are is for her to endorse fatalism. For, if the way in which times are related to one another is necessary, then in every possible world times will be related to each other as they are in the actual world. But, then, in every possible world what is true, was true, and will be true is exactly the same, given the account of these notions developed in Chapter 4. Only what is actually true is possibly true. And this is fatalism. Insofar as fatalism is unattractive, the present objection to the time-ordering story should not move those who would otherwise advocate the story to conclude that it has a very low epistemic status. The prospects are therefore not bad for defending the (at least) not very low epistemic status of the time-ordering story in the face of objections aimed at showing that it involves a bad metaphysics of time.

3.2 Time-ordering and freedom

A second kind of objection to the time-ordering story does not aim to show that its metaphysics of time is internally problematic, but rather aims to show that its metaphysics of time, together with its claim about God's ordering the times, conflicts with the possibility of human freedom. The objector aims to show this not on the basis that the story requires causal determinism, which it plausibly does not, but on the basis that it requires something else which conflicts with the existence of human freedom.

Notably, if an objection of this sort can be made to work, it will threaten the response developed in this book in two ways. First, and most obviously, it will challenge the epistemic status of the time-ordering story given theism. But, second, it will also challenge a key component of the conciliatory story response to the foreknowledge argument. The component it will challenge is the claim that we are in a position to know that the foreknowledge argument is sound only if we are in a position to know that infallible divine foreknowledge requires the truth of causal determinism. This claim was defended on the basis of the idea that the best candidate for that which is both required by infallible divine foreknowledge and explains why human beings lack freedom is the truth of causal determinism. But, if an argument of the sort in view here succeeds, it will identify an alternative good candidate for something that is both required by infallible divine foreknowledge and explains why human beings lack freedom. At least, it will identify a good candidate for something which is required by infallible divine foreknowledge *if* that foreknowledge isn't achieved via causal determinism which would explain why human beings lack freedom.

How could one argue that the metaphysics of the time-ordering story is inconsistent with free human actions, even given that it doesn't require causal determinism? I think there may be several approaches to doing so. What they will have in common is that they identify some metaphysical condition which is plausibly required for there to be free actions but which is arguably ruled out by the metaphysics of the time-ordering story. I'll discuss the prospects of two such approaches here.

The first approach focuses on the Ultimate Sourcehood condition of free action. According to many who work on free will, especially incompatibilists, it is required for an action to be performed freely that its agent be the ultimate source of that action.[2] Often, this condition is spelled out in causal terms, where the action cannot trace back to causal factors beyond the agent herself. The causal buck must stop with her.[3] At least, this is required for those actions for which we are non-derivatively free—those actions which we perform freely, but not because of other actions we freely performed. One might argue that such an Ultimate Sourcehood condition is not satisfied by the time-ordering story. For, as I said in Chapter 5, the time-ordering story permits God's causal activity in ordering the times to explain what happens throughout the course of the world. God's ordering the times as he has offers an explanation for why the grass flattens, for example, at the time following the ball's rolling down the incline. But, similarly, God's causal activity will explain the actions of creatures, including those that are supposed to be non-derivatively free. So, the agents who perform these actions are not the ultimate source of them. The causal source of these actions goes beyond the agents.

I think that developing an objection like this one is a promising way for the opponent of the time-ordering story to challenge that story's consistency with human freedom. But, whether it is ultimately successful will turn on the details of the Ultimate Sourcehood condition. Some ways of spelling out this condition will imply that the time-ordering story is incompatible with human agents being the ultimate sources of their actions; but other ways of spelling out this condition will not have this implication. So, the strength of this objection to the time-ordering story will depend on whether the required conceptions are better than or inferior to alternative conceptions.

Though I cannot offer any decisive considerations here in favor of understanding the Sourcehood condition in such a way that it is not ruled out by the time-ordering story, I will briefly offer a line of thought in favor of this conclusion which might be further developed in the future by an advocate of the time-ordering story. Two competing accounts of the Sourcehood condition are the following:

> Explanatory Sourcehood: For subject S to be the ultimate source of event A, S must be a source of A and there must not be any explanation for A which originates outside of S.
>
> Causal Sourcehood: For subject S to be the ultimate source of event A, S must be a source of A and there must not be causes of A that originate outside of S.

I'll briefly argue here that the time-ordering story is consistent with the satisfaction of the Causal Sourcehood condition; and, I'll argue that there is reason for an incompatibilist to prefer this Sourcehood condition to the Explanatory Sourcehood condition, which cannot be satisfied given the time-ordering story.

---

[2] Two excellent sources for discussion of this condition are Kane (1998) and Timpe (2008).

[3] This is for good reason, I think, since if the Sourcehood condition is stated carefully in causal terms, then it will follow straightway that if causal determinism is true, then the condition cannot be satisfied—something advocates of the condition wish to show. See the way the argument for incompatibilism based on this condition is presented in Timpe (2006b) and Vihvelin (2011).

It should be fairly clear from my remarks in Chapters 4 and 5 that while the time-ordering story is consistent with the Causal Sourcehood condition being satisfied, it is not consistent with the Explanatory Sourcehood condition being satisfied. This is because the time-ordering story is consistent with there being no causes of an event A other than an agent S. But, this can be shown to fulfill the Causal Sourcehood condition because it is not unreasonable to think that when agents agent-cause effects, they are a source of those effects. For example, O'Connor and Jacobs (2013) claim that agents are sources of their acts because they agent-cause their own intentions. The time-ordering story is consistent with this idea; an agent S can agent-cause her intention I to act in some way at a time t. And, she may even do so when there are no other causes of I, including God, as I argued in Chapter 4. Thus, as the time-ordering story is consistent with agents being the source of events which have no other causes, the time-ordering story is consistent with the satisfaction of the Causal Sourcehood condition.[4] It is not compatible with the satisfaction of the Explanatory Sourcehood condition, however, as my claims in Chapter 5 commit me to saying that God's time-ordering activity does provide an explanation for the events that unfold in the history of the world, albeit without causing them. Thus, it is not consistent with the time-ordering story, as I spelled it out, that the intention I, for example, would not have an explanation which originated beyond the agent S.

Notably, there is good reason for the incompatibilist to prefer the Causal Sourcehood condition to the Explanatory Sourcehood condition. This is because nearly any incompatibilist wishes for her view to be consistent with the idea that *reasons* explain an agent's actions. O'Connor and Jacobs take pains to explain how their incompatibilist view is consistent with reasons-explanation, for example. And their effort here is in no way unrepresentative.[5] But, insofar as there are also explanations of why we have the reasons that we do—something these authors wish to permit—it will follow that their views will not satisfy the Explanatory Sourcehood condition. They will permit explanations of an agent's actions which originate beyond the agent. Thus, there is good reason for an incompatibilist to prefer the Causal Sourcehood condition to the Explanatory Sourcehood condition. And, as I've said, the Causal Sourcehood condition can be satisfied by the time-ordering story. Thus, there is reason to be hopeful that the objection to the time-ordering story based on its conflict with agents being the ultimate sources of their acts can be overcome by advocates of the time-ordering story.

A second way to argue that the time-ordering story is incompatible with human freedom is to argue that the time-ordering story does not permit the satisfaction of the Alternative Possibilities condition on free action. If God has ordered the times so that a time t which includes <S does A> as a conjunct is the third time in the world, say, then S cannot do otherwise than A at the third time in the history of the

---

[4]   A similar line of argument can be defended for the ability of the time-ordering story to satisfy the Causal Sourcehood condition given alternative accounts of sourcehood, such as Lowe's (2013) proposal that agents are the source of their willings simply because they are the ones who will.

[5]   See the discussion of reasons-explanation in Clarke and Capes (2013) for an overview of such approaches.

world. But, if S cannot do otherwise than A at the third time, then S's doing A at the third time is not something S does freely.

I think there are two important points for an advocate of the time-ordering strategy to make in response to this argument. The first is that many authors have thought that the Alternative Possibilities condition and the Sourcehood condition are not different conditions. They have thought that if the Sourcehood condition is satisfied, the Alternative Possibilities condition will be satisfied as well and vice versa.[6] If this is correct, then we do not in fact get a distinct second objection to the time-ordering story here. Its success would be tied to the success of the sourcehood objection, for which we already saw there is a promising line of response.

Suppose, however, that the Sourcehood and Alternative Possibilities conditions are distinct and that alternative possibilities are indeed necessary for free action.[7] The second point I think the advocate of the time-ordering story ought to make is the following. In the same way that the plausibility of the sourcehood objection turns on how sourcehood is spelled out, the plausibility of the alternative possibilities objection turns on how the Alternative Possibilities condition is spelled out. And, just as there are various ways of spelling out the Sourcehood condition, some of which can be satisfied by the time-ordering story and some of which cannot be, there are ways of spelling out the Alternative Possibilities condition, some of which can be satisfied by the time-ordering story and some of which cannot be. Thus, the plausibility of the alternative possibilities objection to the time-ordering story rests on defending a version of the Alternative Possibilities condition on free action and showing that this condition cannot be satisfied by the time-ordering story.

With this claim about the plausibility of the alternative possibilities objection in mind, I think there is reason for the advocate of the time-ordering story to be optimistic in the face of this objection. Defending an alternative possibilities condition and showing that it cannot be satisfied by the time-ordering story is a tall order. And, there are conceptions of alternative possibilities, which should be attractive to theists, according to which the time-ordering story *is* compatible with persons being able to do otherwise. For, as I've argued (forthcoming), there is good reason for a theist to think that alternative possibilities are ultimately to be explained by an ontology of powers, as this will make best sense of divine freedom. On such an ontology, at least certain powers are fundamental, not-further-analyzable features of reality. On E. J. Lowe's view, one such power is the will. This power is essentially a two-way power—a power to will and a power to not will. Now, I do not think there is any good reason to think that the time-ordering story cannot permit the existence of such wills. Suppose that at time t, S wills to do A. Thus, t includes <S wills to do A>. Could S have done otherwise? Well, if S's willing consists in his exercising his will, and if the will is essentially a two-way

---

[6] Perhaps the clearest exponent of this view is Kane (2005).

[7] It is important to note that even among those incompatibilists who endorse the Sourcehood condition and distinguish it from the Alternative Possibilities condition, there are those who claim that the Alternative Possibilities condition needn't be satisfied for there to be free action. Advocates of this view are called "narrow source incompatibilists" in (Timpe 2008). For them, the compatibility of the time-ordering story with free will turns only on the sourcehood objection.

power, then yes: S could have willed not to do A. In other words <S has a power to will not do to A> is also a conjunct of t. I see no incoherence here. Thus, I conclude that on at least one conception of alternative possibilities which should be attractive to theists, the time-ordering story can satisfy the Alternative Possibilities condition. There is certainly a good deal of work for the advocate of the alternative possibilities objection to do if she wishes to wield this objection to show that the time-ordering story is of very low epistemic status.

I conclude that while the two objections explored here to the consistency of the time-ordering story with human freedom are powerful and worthy of future investigation, the advocate of the not very low epistemic status of the time-ordering story has reason to be hopeful that such future inquiry may vindicate rather than impugn her view.

3.3 Time-ordering and theodicy

The final objection I will consider to the time-ordering story claims that while the time-ordering story may be consistent with human free will of an incompatibilist sort, its consistency therewith comes at a price the theist should not want to pay. For, it permits human free will in such a way that free will cannot be appealed to in order to help explain why God permits the evils he does in our world. In other words, if the time-ordering story is consistent with human free will, then theists cannot appeal to the existence of free will as part of their effort to present a theodicy. But, as I made clear in Chapter 1, part of the appeal of free will of an incompatibilist sort from the perspective of theism is that such free will is supposed to aid in the presentation of just such a theodicy. Thus, if the time-ordering story is consistent with free will of an incompatibilist sort, it undermines one of the most important motivations the theist has for accepting an incompatibilist account of free will and so is ultimately not attractive given theism.

In order to see the power in this objection, I need to say a bit more about why someone might think that if the time-ordering story is consistent with human freedom of an incompatibilist sort, then human freedom of an incompatibilist sort cannot be appealed to as part of an explanation for why God permits the evils he does in our world. Someone might think this for the following reasons. On the time-ordering story, when God includes times according to which agents will various things in the order of times which constitutes the history of the world, the agents who will as they do at those times thereby satisfy the conditions required for free will we've discussed in this book. Their willing isn't causally determined; they are the ultimate source of their willing; and, they could have willed otherwise. But, this implies that if God wants human beings to exercise free will, all he has to do is include among the order of times which constitutes the world's history times which claim that agents will such-and-such. There is no reason to think that this cannot be done in a way such that none of these times include claims affirming that the kinds of evils which occur in our world occur. Thus, the time-ordering story allows God to construct worlds in which there is free will but no evils like those in our world. The existence of free will therefore cannot be appealed to as part of an explanation for why the evils of our world occur.

Thus, if the time-ordering strategy is consistent with free will of an incompatibilist sort, then the theist will lose one of her central motivations for affirming free will of an incompatibilist sort and so the time-ordering story will lose a good deal of its attractiveness from her perspective.

I again think that there is reason for the advocate of the time-ordering strategy to be hopeful in the face of this objection. There is something the objection gets right about the time-ordering story which may at first appear troubling from the perspective of the theist; but, there is also something important that the objection gets wrong. What the objection gets right is that, given the time-ordering story, it is possible for God to create a world containing free actions without there being evils. To do this, God must simply carefully select times at which persons will various things but at which no evils occur. But, where the objection goes wrong is in concluding on this basis that free will cannot be appealed to as part of an explanation for why God permits the evils of our world.

To see why free will can help to explain the existence of evils in our world given the time-ordering story, we need to turn our attention to something free will is necessary but not sufficient for—namely, moral responsibility. On many approaches to theodicy, what plays a key role in explaining why God permits evils is not simply human beings being able to freely will such-and-such, but rather human beings being able to be morally responsible for bringing about a wide range of good events. On such approaches, a world in which a person S is able to freely will to move S's arms about but in which S is not able to do so in such a way as to be morally responsible for thereby bringing about good states of affairs is, ceteris paribus, less valuable than a world in which S is both able to freely will to move S's arms about *and* able to do so in such a way as to be morally responsible for thereby bringing about various good states of affairs. Theodicies of this sort will not appeal to free will as part of an explanation of the evils of our world on the basis that it is impossible for there to be free willings of the kind which occur in our world without there being such evils. Rather, they will claim that it is impossible for human beings to be capable of being morally responsible for the sorts of goods they are capable of being morally responsible for in our world without there being such evils; and they will claim that persons cannot be morally responsible for anything without there being free will. Free will here plays a role in the explanation of the evils of our world only in that free will is required for making possible something else—wide-ranging moral responsibility—which could not exist without evils like those in our world.

One might worry, however, that this observation only pushes the question one step back. What we were worried about was that an advocate of the time-ordering story would not be able to offer an explanation of (at least some of) the evils of our world partially on the basis of free will. We've clarified two ways one might try to perform this explanation—one way which claims that the existence of free will itself requires the existence of such evils and one way which claims instead that free will is required for something else which requires such evils. We said that the first kind of explanation can't be given by an advocate of the time-ordering story. This is what the objection above was said to have gotten right. But, we haven't yet seen how an advocate of the time-ordering story *can* offer an explanation of the second kind. To put the worry in the form of a question: How could the advocate of the time-ordering story argue that, given her account of time-ordering, wide-ranging moral responsibility will be possible only if there are evils like those that occur in our world?

Here's a brief proposal. First, the advocate of the time-ordering strategy needs to say something about that which is required for wide-ranging moral responsibility apart from free will. The commonly accepted story here, one which is appealed to by both compatibilists and incompatibilists, is that moral responsibility requires not just metaphysical conditions having to do with freedom but also an epistemic condition.[8] For example, suppose that Gus has fired a bullet toward John's brain, but that Sam jumps in front of John taking the bullet from him with the consequence that John survives. For Sam to be morally responsible for the good state of affairs of John's surviving Gus's attack, Sam must meet both certain metaphysical conditions and certain epistemic conditions. Sam must meet metaphysical conditions bearing on his freedom—conditions such as, for example, Sam's being the ultimate source of his leaping or Sam's being able to do otherwise than leap. But, even if Sam satisfies these conditions, he will not be morally responsible for John's survival if he doesn't also meet certain epistemic conditions. How exactly to define these conditions is a matter of significant controversy.[9] But, as a first pass, we might say that Sam will not be morally responsible if he does not hold the reasonable belief that his willing to leap has a decent chance of helping John survive the attack. Swinburne (1998: 183) summarizes the point strikingly, writing that "Free choice without knowledge of effects is empty."

Showing that moral responsibility requires meeting an epistemic condition in addition to meeting metaphysical conditions pertaining to freedom is only the first step toward showing that free will can be appealed to by an advocate of the time-ordering strategy as part of an explanation for why God permits certain evils in our world. A second step is to argue that the epistemic condition required is what I will call a *two-way* epistemic condition. To see what this condition involves, return to the case of Sam. Both compatibilists and incompatibilists will often agree that for Sam to be morally responsible for bringing about John's survival, Sam must have met a two-way metaphysical condition of being able to do otherwise. However, when it comes to the epistemic condition on moral responsibility, it seems strangely to have been overlooked that this condition likewise must be a two-way condition. For example, suppose that Sam believed not only that his willing to leap had a good chance of helping John survive, but that his willing not to leap had equally as good a chance of doing so. Here it seems that Sam is no longer so praiseworthy for saving John when he leaps and his leaping results in John's survival. Sam himself certainly wouldn't have thought he did anything special by leaping here. For, he would have thought that

---

8 Kevin Timpe (2012) writes: "Most extant accounts of moral responsibility…hold that an agent must satisfy two distinct conditions to be morally responsible: a control condition and an epistemic condition."

9 The discussion of this issue is at a nascent stage in comparison with the discussion of the metaphysical conditions on moral responsibility. But, for a good starting point, see Ginet (2001), Vargas (2005), Haji (2008), and Timpe (2012).

whether he willed to jump or willed not to jump, John's survival wouldn't have been affected. Thus, meeting the one-way epistemic condition seems not to be sufficient for moral responsibility when combined with meeting the metaphysical conditions required for moral responsibility. A promising proposal concerning how to address this deficiency in the epistemic condition is to make the epistemic condition a two-way condition. Not only must an agent reasonably believe that her willing, W, may well bring about a state of affairs A for her to be morally responsible for bringing about A by W, but she must reasonably believe that A will not be brought about by her not willing W. In Sam's case, for him to be morally responsible for John's survival, he must not only reasonably believe that his willing to jump has a good chance in resulting in John's survival, but he must reasonably believe that his willing to not jump does not have a good chance in resulting in John's survival. In other words, Sam must reasonably believe that his willing to not jump has a good chance of being followed by John's death.

Thus far, I have only argued that moral responsibility for bringing about good states of affairs, something I am presuming to be of significant value, requires meeting a two-way epistemic condition. Meeting this condition requires agents to have reasonable beliefs about what good *and bad* states of affairs are likely to follow upon their willings. But now only one more step is needed to show how an advocate of the time-ordering story can appeal to free will as part of the explanation for why God permits certain evils in our world. This last step is to argue, following Swinburne (1998), that the best way for God to preside over the world so that creatures satisfy this epistemic condition is for God to permit there to be evils in the world. According to Swinburne, God *could* preside over the world such that agents gain reasonable beliefs about what good and bad states of affairs are likely to follow their willings (say, by the internal testimony of the Spirit about such matters); but, God would prefer not to do this. God would instead prefer that creatures acquire such reasonable beliefs on the basis of induction from past cases—that is, induction from past cases where willings were in fact followed by good and bad states of affairs. Swinburne claims that God would prefer this for a variety of reasons, including the intrinsic value of human learning and the disvalue of God's making his presence too evident to human beings. But, of course, if the reasonable beliefs in question are to be gained on the basis of past cases in which willings were followed by good and bad states of affairs, then there will have to *be* bad past states of affairs. Thus, the best way for God to ensure that human beings have wide-ranging moral responsibility is to permit bad states of affairs. So, if God exercises providence by ordering the times, then if he wishes to create a world in which human beings are morally responsible for certain good states of affairs, he must include in the history of the world some times according to which evils occur. The advocate of the time-ordering story can appeal to free will, then, as a part of a theodicy. Free will is required for moral responsibility, which is itself best accommodated by permitting evils. There is reason for the advocate of the time-ordering strategy to be hopeful that this final objection to the epistemic status of her view based on its undermining the motivation for affirming an incompatibilist conception of freedom is not compelling.

4. Conclusion

After laying out the conciliatory story strategy of responding to the foreknowledge argument in Part I and developing the time-ordering story which implements this strategy in Chapters 4 and 5, I have turned in this chapter to evaluate the combined response to the foreknowledge argument that these afford. My conclusion is that the value of this response is considerable and its future bright. The time-ordering story, and the more general conciliatory story strategy of which it is an implementation, satisfies three criteria for a successful response to the foreknowledge argument which responses to that argument targeting one of its premises or inferences do not satisfy. Furthermore, other simpler responses to the foreknowledge argument which do not involve denying one of its premises or inferences face very significant difficulties. And, finally, there is significant reason for optimism that the most powerful objections to the time-ordering story do not succeed in showing that its epistemic status is very low given theism.

I conclude with a brief remark concerning my hope for this book and with an invitation to my readers. My hope for this book, as I said in the Introduction, is to spur on the community of philosophers of religion to consider more intently the question of *how* divine foreknowledge might be achieved. I have argued here that answering this question is quite important because if there are accounts of how divine foreknowledge might be achieved which do not require causal determinism and which are not of a very low epistemic status given theism, then these accounts can be used to challenge the soundness of the foreknowledge argument. I have attempted to contribute to the stock of such accounts in this book by articulating and defending the time-ordering story discussed in Chapters 4 through 6. It is my contention that this story makes a quite valuable contribution to the relevant stock of conciliatory stories. In light of this, my invitation to my readers is twofold. First, I invite my readers to continue with a rigorous examination of whether the story I have articulated in fact makes the contribution to the stock of needed conciliatory stories that I have proposed it does. I do very much look forward to carrying on continued dialogue about this account of the mechanics of foreknowledge in the future. Second, apart from continuing evaluation of the time-ordering story, I invite my readers to put forward their own best efforts at articulating and evaluating still further conciliatory stories, aiding us all in thinking more carefully and thoroughly about the mechanics whereby God might achieve infallible foreknowledge. As we engage in this project together, it just may be that we come significantly closer to finding successful responses to the age-old questions about the mechanics of divine foreknowledge and providence which have driven the present inquiry.

Bibliography

Adams, Marilyn M. 1967. "Is the Existence of God a 'Hard' Fact?" *Philosophical Review* 76, 4: 492–503.

Adams, Robert M. 1974. "Theories of Actuality." *Nous* 8, 3: 211–31.

———. 1977. "Middle Knowledge and the Problem of Evil." *American Philosophical Quarterly* 14, 2: 109–17.

Almeida, Michael and Graham Oppy. 2003. "Sceptical Theism and Evidential Arguments from Evil." *Australasian Journal of Philosophy* 81, 4: 496–516.

——— and ———. 2004. "Evidential Arguments from Evil and Skeptical Theism." *Philo* 8, 2: 84–94.

Alston, William. 1986. "Does God Have Beliefs?" *Religious Studies* 22, 3/4: 287–306.

———. 1996. "Some (Temporarily) Final Thoughts on the Evidential Argument from Evil." In *The Evidential Argument from Evil*, ed. Daniel Howard-Snyder, 311–32. Bloomington, IN: Indiana University Press.

Audi, Paul. 2012. "Grounding: Toward a Theory of the *In-Virtue-of* Relation." *Journal of Philosophy* 109: 685–711.

Ayer, A. J. 1963. "Fatalism." In *The Concept of a Person and Other Essays*, 235–68. New York: St. Martin's.

Bañez, Domingo, O. P. 1934. *Scholastica Commentaria in Primam Partem Angelici Doctoris Divi Thomas Aquinatis*, ed. Luis Urbano. Madrid: Biblioteca de tomistos espanoles.

Bergmann, Michael. 2001. "Skeptical Theism and Rowe's New Evidential Argument from Evil." *Nous* 35: 278–96.

———. 2009. "Skeptical Theism and the Problem of Evil." In *Oxford Handbook to Philosophical Theology*, ed. Thomas Flint and Michael Rea, 374–99. Oxford: Oxford University Press.

Berto, Francesco. 2009. "Impossible Worlds." In *Stanford Encyclopedia of Philosophy*, ed. Edward N. Zalta. Available online at http://plato.stanford.edu/entries/impossible-worlds/.

Bohm, David and Basil Hiley. 1993. *The Undivided Universe: An Ontological Interpretation of Quantum Tneory*. London: Routledge.

Borland, Tully. 2006. "Omniscience and Divine Foreknowledge." In *Internet Encyclopedia of Philosophy*, ed. James Fieser and Bradley Dowden. Available at http://www.iep.utm.edu/omnisci/.

Bourne, Craig. 2006. *A Future for Presentism*. Oxford: Clarendon Press.

Byerly, T. Ryan 2011. "Ockhamism vs Molinism, Round Two: A Reply to Warfield." *Religious Studies* 47, 4: 503–11.

———. 2012a. "Explaining Away the Prevention Argument for Geachianism." *Ars Disputandi* 12.

———. 2012b. "Why Infallible Divine Foreknowledge cannot Uniquely Threaten Human Freedom, but its Mechanics Might." *European Journal for Philosophy of Religion* 4, 4: 73–94.

———. 2013. "Explanationism and Justified Beliefs about the Future." *Erkenntnis* 78, 1: 229–43.

————. forthcoming. "Foreknowledge, Accidental Necessity, and Uncausability." *International Journal for Philosophy of Religion*.

————. 2014. "God Knows the Future by Ordering the Times." *Oxford Studies in Philosophy of Religion*, vol. 5, ed. Jonathan Kvanvig, Oxford: Oxford University Press, pp.18–39.

Caroll, John. 2010. "Laws of Nature." In *Stanford Encyclopedia of Philosophy*, ed. Edward N. Zalta. Available at http://plato.stanford.edu/entries/laws-of-nature/.

Chisholm, Roderick M. 1976. *Persons and Objects*. La Salle: Open Court.

————. 1977. *Theory of Knowledge*. 2nd ed. Englewood Cliffs: Prentice-Hall.

————. 1979. "Objects and Persons: Revisions and Replies."*Grazer Philosophische Studien* 7, 8: 317–88.

Clarke, Randolph and Justin Capes. 2013. "Incompatibilist (Nondeterminst) Theories of Free Will." In *Stanford Encyclopedia of Philosophy*, ed. Edward Zalta. Available at http://plato.stanford.edu/entries/incompatibilism-theories/.

Clatterbaugh, Kenneth. 1995. "Cartesian Causality, Explanation, and Divine Concurrence." *History of Philosophy Quarterly* 12: 195–206.

Craig, William Lane. 1987. *The Only Wise God*. Grand Rapids: Baker.

————. 1990. *Divine Foreknowledge and Human Freedom. Brill's Studies in Intellectual History 19*. Leiden: E.J. Brill.

————. 2009. "Divine Eternity." In *Oxford Handbook of Philosophical Theology*, ed. Thomas Flint and Michael Rea, 145–66. Oxford: Oxford University Press.

Craig, William and Quentin Smith, eds. 2007. *Einstein, Relativity and Absolute Simultaneity*. London: Routledge.

Crisp, Thomas. 2007. "Presentism and the Grounding Objection." *Nous* 41, 1: 90–107.

Davidson, Matthew. 2003. "Presentism and the Non-Present." *Philosophical Studies* 113, 1: 77–92.

————. 2004. "Critical Notice of Theodore Sider, Four Dimensionalism." *Philosophical Books* 45, 1: 17–33.

Dougherty, Trent and Alexander Pruss. 2014. "Evil and the Problem of Anomaly." *Oxford Studies in Philosophy of Religion* vol.5, ed. Jonathan Kvanvig, 40–70. Oxford: Oxford University Press.

Dvořák, Petr. 2013. "The Concurrentism of Thomas Aquinas: Divine Causation and Human Freedom." *Philosophia* 41, 3: 617–34.

Earman, John. 1986. *A Primer on Determinism*. Dordrecht: Reidel.

Egan, Andy and Brian Weatherson, eds. 2011. *Epistemic Modality*. Oxford: Oxford University Press.

Finch, Alicia and Michael Rea. 2008. "Presentism and Ockham's Way Out." *Oxford Studies in Philosophy of Religion* Vol. I, ed. Jonathan Kvanvig, 1–17. Oxford: Oxford University Press.

———— and Ted Warfield. 1998. "The Mind Argument and Libertarianism." *Mind* 107, 427: 515–28.

Fine, Kit. 2001. "The Question of Realism." *Philosophers' Imprint* 1, 2: 1–30.

———— and Arthur Prior. 1977. *Worlds, Times, and Selves*. Amherst: University of Massachusetts Press.

Fishcher, John M. 1992. "Recent Work on God and Freedom." *American Philosophical Quarterly* 29, 2: 91–109.

————. 2002. "Frankfurt-Style Compatibilism." In *Contours of Agency: Essays on Themes from Harry Frankfurt*, ed. Sarah Buss and Lee Overton, MA: MIT Press: Cambridge, 1–26.

———. 2010. "The Frankfurt Cases: The Moral of the Stories." *Philosophical Review* 119, 3: 315–36.

———, Patrick Todd and Neal Tonazzini. 2009. "Re-reading Nelson Pike's 'Divine Omniscience and Voluntary Action'." *Philosophical Papers* 38, 2: 247–70.

Flint, Thomas. 1998. *Divine Providence: The Molinist Account*. Ithaca: Cornell University Press.

———. 2011. "Whence and Whither the Molinist Debate: A Reply to Hasker." In *Molinism: The Contemporary Debate*, ed. Ken Perszyk, 37–50. Oxford: Oxford University Press.

Frankfurt, Harry. 1969. "Alternate Possibilities and Moral Responsibility." *Journal of Philosophy* 66, 23: 829–39.

Fredosso, Alfred. 1983. "Accidental Necessity and Logical Determinism." *Journal of Philosophy* 80: 257–78.

———. 1988. Translation and Introduction to Luis de Molina *On Divine Foreknowledge* (Part IV of *Concordia*). Ithaca: Cornell University Press.

———. 1991. "God's General Concurrence with Secondary Causes: Why Conservation Is Not Enough." *Philosophical Perspectives* 5: 553–85.

———. 1994. "God's General Concurrence with Secondary Causes: Pitfalls and Prospects." *American Philosophical Quarterly* 67: 131–56.

Geach, Peter. 1977. *Providence and the Problem of Evil*. Cambridge: Cambridge University Press.

Ginet, Carl. 1996. "In Defense of the Principle of Alternate Possibilities: Why I Don't Find Frankfurt's Argument Convincing." *Nous* 30: 403–17.

———. 2001. "The Epistemic Requirements for Moral Responsibility." *Nous* 34, 14: 267–77.

Goetz, Stewart. 2005. "Frankfurt-Style Counterexamples and Begging the Question." *Midwest Studies in Philosophy* 29, 1: 83–105.

Graham, Peter. 2008. "Warfield on Divine Foreknowledge and Human Freedom." *Faith and Philosophy* 25, 1: 75–8.

Haji, Ishtiyaque. 2008. *Moral Responsibility, Authenticity, and Education*. London: Routledge.

Hall, Ned. 2000. "Causation and the Price of Transitivity." *Journal of Philosophy* 97: 198–222.

Hasker, William. 1989. *God, Time, and Knowledge*. Ithaca: Cornell University Press.

———. 1997. "Explanatory Priority: Transitive and Unequivocal, a Reply to William Craig." *Philosophy and Phenomenological Research* 57, 2: 389–93.

———. 1999. *The Emergent Self*. Ithaca: Cornell University Press.

Heil, John. 2012. *The Universe as We Find It*. Oxford: Oxford University Press.

Hoefer, Carl. 2010. "Causal Determinism." In *Stanford Encyclopedia of Philosophy*, ed. Edward N. Zalta. Available at http://plato.stanford.edu/entries/determinism-causal/.

Hoffman, Joshua and Gary Rosenkrantz. 1984. "Hard and Soft Facts." *Philosophical Review* 93, 3: 419–34.

Hunt, David. 1998. "What *Is* the Problem of Theological Fatalism?" *International Philosophical Quarterly* 38, 1: 17–30.

———. 1999. "On Augustine's Way Out." *Faith and Philosophy* 16: 1.

———. 2000. "Moral Responsibility and Unavoidable Action." *Philosophical Studies* 97, 2: 195–227.

Jaworski, William. 2011. *Philosophy of Mind: A Comprehensive Introduction*. Malden, MA: Wiley-Blackwell.

Jenkins, Carrie and Daniel Nolan. 2008. "Backwards Explanation." *Philosophical Studies* 140, 1: 103–15.

Jonathan Lowe, E. 2008. *Personal Agency: The Metaphysics of Mind and Action*. Oxford: Clarendon Press.

———. 2013. "The Will as a Rational Free Power." In *Powers and Capacities in Philosophy: The New Aristotelianism*, ed. R. Groff and J. Greco. London: Routledge, 172–85.

Kane, Robert. 1998. *The Significance of Free Will*. Oxford: Oxford University Press.

———. 2005. *A Contemporary Introduction to Free Will*. New York: Oxford University Press.

Kim, Jaegwon. 1976. "Events as Property Exemplifications." In *Action Theory*, ed. M. Brand and D. Walton, 159–77. Dordrecht: Reidel.

———. 2005. *Physicalism, or Something Near Enough*. Princeton: Princeton University Press.

Korman, Daniel Z. 2011. "Ordinary Objects." In *The Stanford Encyclopedia of Philosophy*, ed. Edward N. Zalta. Available at http://plato.stanford.edu/entries/ordinary-objects/.

Kriegel, Uriah. 2009. *Subjective Consciousness: A Self-representational Theory*. Oxford: Oxford University Press.

Kvanvig, Jonathan. 2003. *The Value of Knowledge and the Pursuit of Understanding*. Cambridge: Cambridge University Press.

———. 2007. "Creation and Conservation." In *The Stanford Encyclopedia of Philosophy*, ed. Edward N. Zalta. Avalable at http://plato.stanford.edu/entries/creation-conservation/.

———. 2011. *Destiny and Deliberation: Essays in Philosophical Theology*. Oxford: Oxford University Press.

———. 2013. "Theories of Creation and Providence." *Res Philosophica* 90, 1: 51–69.

Lange, Marc. 2013. "Grounding, Scientific Explanation, and Humean Laws." *Philosophical Studies* 164, 1: 255–61.

Lewis, David. 1973. *Counterfactuals*. Oxford: Blackwell.

———. 1996. "Elusive Knowledge." *Australasian Journal of Philosophy* 74, 4: 549–67.

Lucas, John. 1989. *The Future: An Essay on God, Temporality, and Truth*. Oxford: Blackwell.

Makinson, D. C. 1965. "The Paradox of the Preface." *Analysis* 25: 205–7.

Mancha, Louis. 2001. *Concurrentism: A Philosophical Explanation*. Unpublished doctoral dissertation.

Markosian, Ned. 2008. "Time." In *Stanford Encyclopedia of Philosophy*, ed. Edward N. Zalta. Available at http://plato.stanford.edu/entries/time/.

———. 2012. "Agent Causation as the Solution to All the Compatibilist's Problems." *Philosophical Studies* 157, 3: 383–98.

McBrayer, Justin. 2009. "CORNEA and Inductive Evidence." *Faith and Philosophy* 26, 1: 77–86.

———. 2010. "Skeptical Theism." *Philosophy Compass* 4, 1: 1–13.

McCall, Storrs. 2011. "The Supervenience of Truth: Freewill and Omniscience." *Analysis* 71: 501–6.

McCann, Hugh. 1995. "Divine Sovereignty and the Freedom of the Will." *Faith and Philosophy* 12, 4: 582–98.

McGrew, Timothy. 2006. "Has Plantinga Refuted the Historical Argument?" *Philosophia Christi* 6: 7–26.

McGrew, Timothy and Lydia McGrew. 2008. "On the Historical Argument: A Rejoinder to Plantinga." *Philosophia Christi* 8, 1: 23–38.

McKay, Thomas and David Johnson. 1996. "A Reconsideration of an Argument against Compatibilism." *Philosophical Topics* 24: 113–22.

McKenna, Michael and David Widerker, eds. 2006. *Moral Responsibility and Alternative Possibilities*. Burlington, VT: Ashgate.

McMullin, Ernan. 1993. "Evolution and Special Creation." *Zygon* 28: 299–335.

McTaggart, J. M. E. 1993. "The Unreality of Time." In *The Philosophy of Time*, ed. Robin Le Poidevin and Murray McBeath, 23–34. Oxford: Oxford University Press. 1993.

Mellor, D. H. 1995. *The Facts of Causation*. London: Routledge.

Menzel, Christopher. 1987. "Theism, Platonism, and the Metaphysics of Mathematics." *Faith and Philosophy* 4, 4: 365–82.

Menzies, Peter. 2008. "Counterfactual Theories of Cuasation." In *Stanford Encyclopedia of Philosophy*, ed. Edward N. Zalta. Available at http://plato.stanford.edu/entries/causation-counterfactual/.

Merricks, Trenton. 2001. *Objects and Persons*. Oxford: Oxford University Press.

——. 2003. "Replies." *Philosophy and Phenomenological Research* 67, 3: 212–33.

——. 2009. "Truth and Freedom." *The Philosophical Review* 118: 29–57.

——. 2011a. "Foreknowledge and Freedom." *The Philosophical Review* 120: 567–86.

——. 2011b. "Truth and Molinism." In *Molinism: The Contemporary Debate*, ed. Ken Perszyk. Oxford: Oxford University Press, 50–72.

Miller, Timothy. 2011. "Continuous Creation and Secondary Causation: The Threat of Occasionalism." *Religious Studies* 47, 1: 3–22.

Minkowski, H. 1952. "Space and Time." Reprinted and translated in *The Principle of Relativity*, ed. Frances Davies and Albert Einstein, 73–91. New York City: Dover Publications.

Molina Luis de, S. J. 1988. *Liberi Arbitrii cum Gratiae Donis, Divina Prascientia, Providentia, Praedestinatione et Reprobatione Concordia*, trans. Alfred Freddoso, ed. Johann Rabeneck and S.J. Oña in *On Divine Foreknowledge: Part IV of the Concordia*, Ithaca; Madrid: Cornell .

Monton, Bradley. forthcoming. "God Acts in the Quantum World." In *Oxford Studies in Philosophy of Religion*, vol. 5, ed. Jonathan Kvanvig. Oxford: Oxford University Press, pp. 133–46.

Morris, Thomas. 1987. *Anselmian Explorations*. Notre Dame: Notre Dame.

Mumford, Stephen and Rani Anjum. 2011. *Getting Causes from Powers*. Oxford: Oxford University Press.

Murphy, Nancey. 2009. "Divine Action in the Natural Order: Buridan's Ass and Schrodinger's Cat." In *Philosophy, Science and Divine Action*, ed. F. LeRon Shults, Nancey C. Murphy and Robert J. Russell, 263–304. Leiden: Brill.

Ney, Alyssa. 2013. "Introduction." In *The Wave Function: Essays in the Metaphysics of Quantum Mechanics*, ed. A. Ney and D. Albert. Oxford: Oxford University Press.

O'Connor, Timothy. 2000. *Persons and Causes: The Metaphysics of Free Will*. Oxford: Oxford University Press.

—— and Jonathan Jacobs. 2013. "Agent-Causation in a Neo-Aristotelian Metaphysics." In *Mental Causation and Ontology*, ed. S. C. Gibb, E. J. Lowe and R. D. Ingthorrson, 173–92. Oxford: Oxford University Press.

Padgett, Alan. 2012. "The Difference Creation Makes: Relative Timelessness Reconsidered." In *God, Eternity and Time*, ed. Christian Tapp and Edmund Runggaldier. Burlington, VT: Ashgate.

Pereboom, Derk. 2001. *Living Without Free Will*. Cambridge: Cambridge University Press.

Pessin, Andrew. 2003. "Descartes's Nomic Concurrentism: Finite Causation and Divine Concurrence."*Journal of the History of Philosophy* 41, 1: 25–49.

Plantinga, Alvin. 1974a. *God, Freedom, and Evil*. New York: Harper and Row.

———. 1974b. *The Nature of Necessity*. Oxford: Oxford University Press.

———. 1986. "On Ockham's Way Out." *Faith and Philosophy* 3, 3: 235–69.

———. 1988. "Epistemic Probability and Evil." *Archivo di filosofia* 56: 557–84.

———. 2000. *Warranted Christian Belief*. Oxford: Oxford University Press.

———. 2006. "Historical Arguments and Dwindling Probabilities: A Response to Timothy McGrew." *Philosophia Christi* 8: 23–38.

Price, H. H. 1950. *Perception, 2nd ed*. London: Methuen.

Prior, Arthur. 1996. "A Statement of Temporal Realism." In *Logic and Reality: Essays on the Legacy of Arthur Prior*, ed. B. J. Copeland, 45–46. Oxford: Clarendon Press.

Pruss, Alexander. 2006. *The Principle of Sufficient Reason: A Reassessment*. Cambridge: Cambridge University Press.

———. 2010. "Probability and the Open Future View." *Faith and Philosophy* 27, 2: 190–6.

———. 2011. "From Restricted to Full Omniscience." *Religious Studies* 47: 257–64.

———. 2012. "A Counterexample to Plantinga's Free Will Defense." *Faith and Philosophy* 29, 4: 400–15.

Rhoda, Alan. 2007. "The Philosophical Case for Open Theism." *Philosophia* 35, 3/4: 301–11.

———. 2008. "Generic Open Theism and Some Varieties Thereof." *Religious Studies* 44, 2: 225–34.

———. 2010. "Probability, Truth, and the Openness of the Future." *Faith and Philosophy* 27, 2: 197–204.

———, Gregory Boyd and Thomas Belt. 2006. "Open Theism, Omniscience, and the Nature of the Future." *Faith and Philosophy* 23, 4: 432–59.

Rota, Michael. 2010. "The Eternity Solution to the Problem of Human Freedom and Divine Foreknowledge." *European Journal of Philosophy of Religion* 2, 1: 165–86.

Rowe, William L. 1979. "The Problem of Evil and Some Varieties of Atheism." *American Philosophical Quarterly* 16: 335–41.

Rudder Baker, Lynn. 2003. "Why Christians Should Not Be Libertarians: An Augustinian Challenge." *Faith and Philosophy* 20, 4: 460–78.

Russell, Bertrand. 1912. "On the Notion of Cause." *Proceedings of the Aristotelian Society* 13: 1–26.

Russell, Robert John. 2009. "Divine Action and Quantum Mechanics: A Fresh Assessment." In *Philosophy, Science and Divine Action*, ed. F. LeRon Shults, Nancey C. Murphy and Robert J. Russell, 351–404. Leiden: Brill.

Saunders, John T. 1966. "Of God and Freedom." *Philosophical Review* 74: 219–75.

Schaffer, Jonathan. 2007. "The Metaphysics of Causation." In *Stanford Encyclopedia of Philosophy*, ed. Edward N. Zalta. Available at http://plato.stanford.edu/entries/causation-metaphysics/.

Sennett, James. 1993. "The Inscrutable Evil Defense against the Inductive Argument from Evil." *Faith and Philosophy* 10: 220–9.

Sider, Theodore. 2003. "What's So Bad about Overdetermination?" *Philosophy and Phenomenological Research* 67, 3: 719–26.

———. 2010. *Logic for Philosophy*. Oxford: Oxford University Press.

Stump, Eleonore. 1999. "Alternative Possibilities and Moral Responsibility: The Flicker of
    Freedom." *Journal of Ethics* 3: 299–324.
———. 2001. "Augustine and Free Will." In *The Cambridge Companion to Augustine*, ed.
    Eleonore Stump and Norman Kretzman. Cambridge: Cambridge University Press,
    124–47.
——— and Norman Kretzmann. 1981. "Eternity." *Journal of Philosophy* 78 (August):
    429–58.
Suarez, Francisco. 1965. *Opera Omnia: Nova Editio*, vols. 25 and 26, ed. Carolo Berton.
    Hildesheim.
Swinburne, Richard. 1998. *Providence and the Problem of Evil*. Oxford: Oxford University
    Press.
———. 2004. "Natural Theology, Its 'Dwindling Probabilities' and 'Lack of Rapport.'" *Faith
    and Philosophy* 21, 4: 533–46.
Talbott, Thomas. 1986. "On Divine Foreknowledge and Bringing About the Past."
    Philosophy and Phenomenological Research 46: 455–69.
Timpe, Kevin. 2006a. "A Critique of Frankfurt-Libertariansim." *Philosophia* 34, 2:
    189–202.
———. 2006b. "The Dialectical Role of Flickers of Freedom." *Philosophical Studies* 131, 2:
    337–68.
———. 2008. *Free Will: Sourcehood and Its Alternatives*. New York: Continuum.
———. 2012. "Tracing and the Epistemic Condition on Moral Responsibility." *Modern
    Schoolman* 88, 1/2: 5–28.
Todd, Patrick. 2011. "Geachianism." *Oxford Studies in Philosophy of Religion, Vol. 3*, ed.
    Jonathan L. Kvanvig. Oxford: Oxford University Press, 222–51.
———. 2013. "Soft Facts and Ontological Dependence." *Philosophical Studies* 164, 3:
    829–44.
Tooley, Michael. 1991. "The Argument from Evil." *Philosophical Perspectives* 5: 89–134.
———. 2008. "Does God Exist?" In *Knowledge of God*, ed. Alvin Plantinga. Oxford:
    Blackwell, 70–150.
———. 2012. "The Problem of Evil." In *Stanford Encyclopedia of Philosophy*, ed. Edward N.
    Zalta. Available at http://plato.stanford.edu/entries/evil/.
Tracy, Thomas. 2009. "Creation, Providence, and Quantum Chance." In *Philosophy, Science
    and Divine Action*, ed. F. LeRon Shults, Nancey C. Murphy and Robert J. Russell,
    227–62. Leiden: Brill.
Trakakis, Nick. 2003. "Evil and the Complexity of History: A Response to Durston."
    Religious Studies 39, 4: 451–58.
Van Inwagen, Peter. 1983. *An Essay on Free Will*. Oxford: Clarendon.
———. 2008. "What Does an Omniscient Being Know about the Future?" *Oxford Studies
    in Philosophy of Religion, Vol. 1*, ed. Jonathan L. Kvanvig. Oxford: Oxford University
    Press, 216–30.
Vander Laan, David. 2004. "Counterpossibles and Similarity." *Lewisian Themes: The
    Philosophy of David K. Lewis*, ed. Jackson and Priest. Oxford: Oxford University Press.
Vargas, Manuel. 2005. "The Trouble with Tracing." *Midwest Studies in Philosophy* 29,
    1: 269–91.
Vihvelin, Kadri. 2011. "Arguments for Incompatibilism." In *Stanford Encyclopedia
    of Philosophy*, ed. Edward Zalta. Available at http://plato.stanford.edu/entries/
    incompatibilism-arguments/.

Wainwright, William J. 2001. "Theological Determinism and the Problem of Evil: Are Arminians Any Better Off?" *International Journal for Philosophy of Religion* 50, 1/3: 81–96.

Warfield, Ted. 1997. "Divine Foreknowledge and Human Freedom are Compatible." *Nous* 31, 1: 80–6.

———. 2000. "On Freedom and Foreknowledge: A Reply to Two Critics." *Faith and Philosophy* 17 (April): 255–59.

———. 2010. "Ockhamism and Molinism—Foreknowledge and Prophecy." In *Oxford Studies in Philosophy of Religion, Vol. 2*, ed. Jonathan L. Kvanvig. Oxford: Oxford University Press, 317–32.

Westphal, Jonathan. 2011. "The Compatibility of Divine Foreknowledge and Freewill." *Analysis* 71: 246–52.

Whipple, John. 2010. "Leibniz on Divine Concurrence." *Philosophy Compass* 5, 10: 865–79.

Widerker, David. 1995. "Libertarianism and Frankfurt's Attack on the Principle of Alternative Possibilities." *Philosophical Review* 104, 2: 247–61.

Wierenga, Edward. 2007. "Perfect Goodness and Divine Freedom." *Philosophical Books* 48, 3: 207–16.

Wilks, Ian. 2009. "Skeptical Theism and Empirical Unfalsifiability." *Faith and Philosophy* 26, 1: 64–76.

Wykstra, Stephen. 1984. "The Humean Obstacle to Evidential Arguments from Suffering: On Avoiding the Evils of 'Appearance'." *International Journal of Philosophy of Religion* 16: 73–93.

———. 2007. "Cornea, Closure, and Current Closure Beffudlement." *Faith and Philosophy* 24, 1: 87–98.

Zagzebski, Linda. 1996. *The Dilemma of Freedom and Foreknowledge*. Oxford: Oxford University Press.

———. 2000. "Does Libertarian Freedom Require Alternative Possibilities?" *Philosophical Perspectives* 14: 231–48.

———. 2011. "Foreknowledge and Free Will." In *Stanford Encyclopedia of Philosophy*, ed. Edward N. Zalta. Available at http://plato.stanford.edu/entries/free-will-foreknowledge/.

———. 2012. "Eternity and Fatalism." In *God, Eternity, and Time*, ed. Christian Tapp and Edmund Runggaldier. Burlington, VT: Ashgate, 65–80.

Zalta, Edward N. 1983. *Abstract Objects: An Introduction to Axiomatic Metaphysics*. Dordrecht: D. Reidel.

———. 1987. "On the Structural Similarities between Worlds and Times." *Philosophical Studies* 51, 2: 213–59.

Zemach, Eddy M. and David Widerker. 1987. "Facts, Freedom, and Foreknowledge." *Religious Studies* 23: 19–28.

Index